Welcome Home

A Guide to Homemaking,

From the Heart

Gina Romero

This Book is Dedicated to You

Welcome Home

A Guide to Homemaking,

From the Heart

Gina Romero

WELCOME HOME: A Guide to Homemaking, From the Heart by Gina Romero
Copyright © 2025 by Gina Romero
All Rights Reserved.
ISBN: 978-1-59755-857-0
Published by: ADVANTAGE BOOKS™
Saint Johns, FL USA
www.advbookstore.com

All Rights Reserved. This book and parts thereof may not be reproduced in any form, stored in a retrieval system or transmitted in any form by any means (electronic, mechanical, photocopy, recording or otherwise) without prior written permission of the author, except as provided by United States of America copyright law.

Scriptures taken from THE HOLY BIBLE, ENGLISH STANDARD VERSION® Copyright© 2001 by Crossway, a publishing ministry of Good News Publishers. Used by permission.

Library of Congress Catalog Number: 2025944710

Names:	Romero, Gina
Title:	WELCOME HOME: *A Guide to Homemaking, From the Heart*
	Gina Romero, Author
	Advantage Books, 2025
Identifiers:	ISBN Paperback: 9781597558570
	ISBN Hardcover: 9781597558471
Subjects:	ISBN eBook: 9781597558716
	Christian Life - Inspirational

First Edition Published November 2025
25 26 27 28 29 30 31   10 9 8 7 6 5 4 3 2

Introduction

Hello Dear Reader,

I'm so glad this book has made its way into your hands. Whether thumbing through these pages because you're interested in homemaking, or because you're thinking of your daughter, sister, mother, niece, aunt, or best friend, I'm so glad you're here, *Welcome Home*.

I wrote this book for Christian women who juggle the demands of work- whether inside the home or outside of it (and often both!) -to share the lessons I've learned and offer timeless, tasteful inspiration on everything from gardening and crafting to cooking, cleaning, and home decorating.

As the years have gone by, I have found increasing joy in the art and science of homemaking. I define homemaking as a catch-all term for all the thoughtful and meaningful special moments and memories we curate for our families. Those can start with the curb appeal of your family home and the garden you've poured yourself into in stolen moments as your family arrives home after baseball games or horseback riding lessons. Those moments are included in the dedication you show when you work to make that homemade meal for your family's dinner while you supervise homework. They're in the joy you find in hand-crafting experiences and making everyday moments special for your family. It's the cleaning you do that no one else on earth can see, yet there you are at 10pm with a magic eraser on your way to bed from the kitchen with a glass of water. And of course, its those precious holidays when you're weary from Christmas gift wrapping for hours or stuffing dozens and dozens of Easter eggs, only to wake up in the morning to put together a brioche French toast casserole brunch for your family.

I have found that being a mother is the hardest job I've ever had, and trust me, I have had some wicked hard jobs. But I crawl into bed at night with a sense of joy and fulfillment. So, I wanted to share what I love the most with you. Coming to you as a flawed and imperfect student of my craft, I seek to offer you the best of what I know in the beautiful, joyful, and fastidious world of homemaking.

I know what it's like to have roles and responsibilities (and dare I say goals) both outside of the home in the world of work, as well as inside the home among my husband and children. I know firsthand the challenges of being a working girl with limited time and a finite budget, and yet the role to which we women are called in the Kingdom is astoundingly rigorous. As both an inspiration and, truthfully, an aspiration- for myself and for you, dear reader, I've included in the pages that follow the passage known as the "Proverbs 31 Woman". This excerpt from the 31st chapter of Proverbs comes from the sayings of King Lemuel, taught to him by his mother. May we run this race with grace and strength, rising to the challenge each step of the way.

For His Glory,
Gina

"Therefore, since we are surrounded by such a great cloud of witnesses, let us throw off everything that hinders and the sin that so easily entangles. And let us run with perseverance the race marked out for us, fixing our eyes on Jesus, the pioneer and perfecter of faith." Hebrews 12:1-2

The Proverbs 31 Woman

"Who can find a virtuous and capable wife?
She is more precious than rubies.
Her husband can trust her, and she will greatly enrich his life.
She brings him good, not harm, all the days of her life.
She finds wool and flax and busily spins it.
She is like a merchant's ship, bringing her food from afar.

She gets up before dawn to prepare breakfast for her household and plan the day's work for her servant girls.
She goes to inspect a field and buys it; with her earnings she plants a vineyard.
She is energetic and strong, a hard worker.
She makes sure her dealings are profitable; her lamp burns late into the night.
Her hands are busy spinning thread, her fingers twisting fiber.
She extends a helping hand to the poor and opens her arms to the needy.
She has no fear of winter for her household, for everyone has warm clothes.
She makes her own bedspreads. She dresses in fine linen and purple gowns.

Her husband is well known at the city gates, where he sits with the other civic leaders.
She makes belted linen garments and sashes to sell to the merchants.
She is clothed with strength and dignity, and she laughs without fear of the future.
When she speaks, her words are wise, and she gives instructions with kindness.
She carefully watches everything in her household and suffers nothing from laziness.

Her children stand and bless her. Her husband praises her: 'There are many virtuous and capable women in the world, but you surpass them all!'
Charm is deceptive, and beauty does not last; but a woman who fears the Lord
will be greatly praised.
Reward her for all she has done.
Let her deeds publicly declare her praise."

Proverbs 31:10-31

Table of Contents

Introduction 5
The Proverbs 31 Woman 7
CHAPTER 1: LANDSCAPING & GARDENING 11
CHAPTER 2: HOME & GARAGE ORGANIZATION 19
CHAPTER 3: INTERIOR DESIGN & DÉCOR 27
CHAPTER 4: CLEANING & CARE 33
CHAPTER 5: HOSTING 47
CHAPTER 6: TABLESCAPES 65
CHAPTER 7: IN THE KITCHEN 75
    Appetizers 79
    Salads & Dressings 83
    Mains 89
    Poultry 90
    Beef 94
    Pork 96
    Fish 99
    Pastas 101
    Vegetarian & Vegan 104
    Soups & Stews 106
    Desserts 109
    Pies 111
    Muffins 113
    Cookies 115
    Brownies 119
    Cakes 120
    Cupcakes 125
    Beverages 128
    Breads 130
    Breakfasts 134
CHAPTER 8: ODDS & ENDS 139
Reflection Questions 149
Resources 157
Acknowledgements 161
About the Author 162

Welcome Home: *A Guide to Homemaking From the Heart*

Chapter 1
Landscaping & Gardening

"There is a time for everything, and a season for every activity under the heavens: a time to be born and a time to die, a time to plant and a time to uproot, a time to kill and a time to heal, a time to tear down and a time to build, a time to weep and a time to laugh, a time to mourn and a time to dance, a time to scatter stones and a time to gather them, a time to embrace and a time to refrain from embracing, a time to search and a time to give up, a time to keep and a time to throw away, a time to tear and a time to mend, a time to be silent and a time to speak, a time to love and a time to hate, a time for war and a time for peace.

What do workers gain from their toil? I have seen the burden God has laid on the human race. He has made everything beautiful in its time He has also set eternity in the human heart; yet no one can fathom what God has done from beginning to end. I know that there is nothing better for people than to be happy and to do good while they live. That each of them may eat and drink and find satisfaction in all their toil- this is the gift of God. I know that everything God does will endure forever; nothing can be added to it and nothing taken from it." Ecclesiastes 3:1-14

In the spring everything bursts into bloom, not unlike our senses.

I often feel closest to God when I'm gardening. It's one of the few things I do where I can lose track of time and get truly lost in it, a much needed solace in this fast-paced world driven by time constraints and deadlines. He was after all, the original gardener. I have often mused as to what the Garden of Eden looked like, smelled like, felt like, and tasted like. A glorious treasure trove of God's most glorious goodness. Flowers, plants and trees of every kind and variety, fruits in a wealthy array of colors, tastes, and textures, and fresh, sunkissed vegetables rich in phytochemicals and nutrients.

I had a pain management specialist tell me once that food is medicine. Fresh produce boosts the immune system, may reduce the risk of stroke, cancer, heart disease, high blood pressure, diabetes and other chronic conditions. The power packed goodness of fresh fruits and vegetables are truly gifts from God. For antioxidants, fiber, anti-inflammatory properties, and so much more, go to fresh fruits and veggies first before you reach for pills (supplements).

I live in Southern California, where we don't have to worry much about preparing our landscaping or flower beds like other parts of the nation.

No, when thinking about gardening and preparing to plant, the only worry I truly have is: *will this plant make it through Labor Day weekend*? (Our hottest time of the year where temperatures can easily be in excess of 110°F, and I'm always left with a few casualties, much to my chagrin.)

I'm pleased to say that I'm able to maintain my gardens and landscaping for less than a hundred dollars a year (excluding the cost of water) and most of that cost comes from the specialty (slow release, citrus-tree-specific) fertilizer I buy. I do save a lot of money by composting and enriching my soil that way. (See Chapter 8 for my downloadable Composting Guide.)

So, for the mamas who are short on time and budget, I'd like to share with you how I do it. I had the opportunity to gain a lot deeper breadth and depth of experience in this area in just the last few years. When we acquired our home in 2018, there was only hardscaping in front and back, and two raised planter beds for vegetable gardening. My family had to overhaul the landscaping, design, softscape composition, built elements, and create environmental sustainability.

While I was out on maternity leave, and my daughter was in the NICU, I moonlighted as a landscape architect for my next door neighbor which was such a blessing to me. I needed a respite and a distraction from the traumatic and very scary world of micro-prematurity (she was born at 27 weeks at 1 pound and 11 inches), severe growth restriction, oxygen liters, IVs, brain scans, bowel failure, and more.

I think the most important thing to bear in mind while you get the feel for your yard and your soil type is the fact that planting a garden of any kind is a trial-and-error process.

The Soil Test

To determine the type of soil you're working with (and it can be different from your front yard to your backyard or side yard) do an at-home sediment test. All you need is a mason jar and soap. Put a handful of soil in the jar with 1 tablespoon of dish soap. Then fill the jar with water, shake, and allow it to sit / settle down. Soil elements settle in this order: sand, silt, organic matter, and clay. Larger or more dense particles (such as sand and organic matter) will settle quickly, but you'll need your jar to sit, unmoved, for up to one week in order to get the most accurate results of your soil test, as smaller components such as clay will take at least a week to settle. Once the water is clear and you can identify distinct layers visually, measure the height of all the soil, then measure each layer. The height of each layer ÷ the total height of the soil = dominant soil type.

Even though I did all my research and was as prepared as I could possibly be to install the right types of plants and flowers for the various areas of my yard rich in clay, or sand, I still experienced defeat. Gardens require patience and understanding. Not every plant will perform exactly as its tag says it will in an area of your yard, so you'll learn as you go, but expect to have an experience of trial and failure. And that's ok!

Zones

Researching the USDA plant hardiness zone you're in is an excellent task to help ensure success. From there think about what you love and would like to see every day. What brings your heart joy? Do you want perennials that have seeds you can save and use year after year? Do you want succulents that need little water and maintenance? Also consider the time of year that is ideal for planting where you live. My daughter was born in March, which is the beginning of spring in Southern California, so I lucked out when embarking upon my neighbor's landscaping project. As I went about working the earth to prepare it for new life and trimming and pruning existing greenery, I prayed to the Lord thanking him for the life of my daughter, bringing before him my fears, anxieties and requests. God is good. Now people often think of spring as the only planting season, however, autumn can be a fabulous runner up. While the air may begin to cool with the arrival of fall, dirt (and water for that matter) remain warm from their season in the unabashed sunshine. Warm soil is ideal for new root growth, so take advantage of two planting seasons in the year if you can.

Scale

Scale is a fundamental principle in garden planning because it ensures that all elements- plants, structures, and pathways- are proportionate to each other and to the overall space. A well-scaled garden feels balanced and harmonious, allowing for both visual interest and functional use. Without careful attention to scale, a garden can feel either cluttered and overwhelming, or sparse and underwhelming. Larger plants go in the back, medium size plants go in the middle, and smaller plants and flowers go along the border of the garden bed.

It's very important to do your research before buying anything. Even a single-family home's yard has microclimates (shade, sun, wind, varying soil acidities, and/or water features). Maintaining your plants and flowers while you navigate the patchwork quilt of your garden's microclimates provides a fun challenge, and you don't have to spend a fortune.

Speaking of spending, you do want to invest in proper gear. My husband, who is the polar opposite of me (patient, methodical, unrushed, pensive) always says that there's a tool for every job, and I agree with him. First, you'll want to get a crate, hard sided tote, or another type of carrier to transport things from one area to another. Personally, I have difficulty stopping long enough to put on an apron, but you should get an apron, a proper pair of gardening shoes (that may look like waterproof sandals, rain boots, clogs, or whatever is conducive to your area). I'm usually barefoot (do as I say, not as I do). Similarly, gloves are a must. Every two weeks I give myself a gel manicure and that polish has to last as long as it humanly, possibly can, so I glove up. You'll also need a watering can, shears, pruners, and a small shovel. You can get most of these things at your local garden store. I like shopping with Armstrong Garden Centers and Greenthumb, as they are fabulous retailers with quality products.

Soil

Typically, you have to prepare your soil; digging to loosen compaction and aerate the soil so it can take on root development and soak up water properly. You will also want to add a soil fertilizer as the sun bakes soil and the nutrients dissipate due to weathering. Happily, there are a whole host of perennials that enjoy a lean soil such as blanket flower, butterfly weed, lavender, and Russian sage.

Water

There is a plethora of ways to get water to your garden; hoses, sprinklers, drip systems, hand watering, etc. My suggestion is to begin with the end in mind and plan out your watering method(s) before you get started. For as much as I love it, container gardening is really a hit or miss for me if I'm relying on hand watering. A drip system on a timer works much better for me, because sometimes I have to travel for work, or there are ten million other priorities vying for my attention, and hand watering just doesn't happen. I use the B-hyve app on my phone to handle the watering for the majority of my yard, and I am obsessed with it! I can literally get in the car to go to work, or to pick up kids from school and with the push of a button, water my yard. It's a game changer.

Conversely, if you have mostly hardscape or lawn at your house but you aspire to garden, consider a raised planter bed or container garden. Just a little wisdom on raised planter beds, if you want them to last year-in and year-out, I do not recommend investing in wood as they are most susceptible to weathering. Metal planter beds are far more durable, yet at the same time, I would also recommend installing a drip watering system in them as they conduct and retain heat and that can dry out your soil quickly. No matter what type of landscaping or gardening you're working with, just be realistic about the amount of time you have that you can spare on such an extracurricular activity. Additionally, if you plan to enjoy a container garden, consider the different materials of containers for what you're planting. For example, terracotta is a very common container, but it does not retain water and is prone to freezing so it's best to consider your zone, and plant anything that's drought tolerant in terracotta. Ceramic containers, however, are safe to use if your zone freezes. Self-watering containers are fabulous to use if you want to enjoy a garden but fear you won't have enough time to keep things alive. These are usually plastic and are equipped with a reservoir and holes drilled in the bottom of the pot so the roots can suck up moisture from the reservoir tray. To ensure free drainage, it's best to put such pots up on plant risers.

And if you don't have a yard, don't let that stop you! Urban gardening is amazing and can be done with a balcony or a kitchen windowsill that gets sunlight. For this type of space, consider a delightful herb garden and enjoy mint, basil, rosemary, oregano and sage to name only a few, right in your kitchen! Another positive thing about an herb garden is that herbs don't need to be fertilized. At most, feeding once during their growing season while they're getting established is enough.

When installing your garden, think about repetitive elements, such as iceberg roses (always plant in odd numbers, such as 3 or 5 of them) and singular elements (such as a bird house or bench), which would complement the garden, but need to be installed on their own. I recommend buying the bigger version of the plant, flower, or shrub you'd like to install in your yard. The reason for this is because gardening is a lesson in patience, and it will take likely at least a year for your plant to mature into the big, bodacious wonder you know it can be. These will be a little more expensive than the smaller versions, but worth it in the short run.

Admittedly, I am not a very big "fussy flower" gardener (I get testy with flowers that give me attitude), but I am very big on aesthetics. In my garden I have married hearty flora that you can't kill, with succulents that reproduce.

Very hearty flora I highly recommend are lantana, iceberg roses, hibiscus, morning glory, bougainvillea, lavender, Jerusalem sage, pride of Madeira, and geraniums. I'd like to pause for a moment at geraniums. Geraniums are amazing. They come in so many vibrant colors (pink, white, red, peach, and more) and not only are they hearty little soldiers, but all you have to do to get a whole new flower to plant is snip off a branch, replant, and watch it grow! Because the quality is so good, I love buying roses from Heirloom Roses(.com). When my baby was first home from the NICU and still medically fragile, there was no time or bandwidth for me to get to my local garden store, but I could order some roses online in the waiting room of the Pediatric Pulmonologist's office while she slept. Heirloom Roses are such quality blooms and ship beautifully to your home. Some of the roses I've purchased from them and highly recommend are; velvet fragrance, double delight, perfume factory, just joey, and iceberg. Most of my roses are the iceberg variety. These roses are known as shrub roses, so they go well along a fence or by a gate (if not installing climbing roses). Shrub roses are often the best choice for new gardeners as they are both tough and healthy (disease resistant) and easily produce beautiful blooms year round while needing minimal maintenance. Keeping your rosebushes and plants safe from pests and health is easy enough too. A mild solution of dish soap and water in a spray bottle is all you need to ward off intruders. And, the benefit of this homemade method is that it's pretty organic. (Often pesticides end up getting rid of more than just pests and can harm pollinators.)

I like to incorporate the use of succulents into my gardens too because they can reproduce with a single snip and replant, are drought tolerant, and come in the widest array of textures, shapes, colors, and they flower.

Every spring, I watch the hummingbirds suckle nectar from my aloe's golden blossoms and I pause for a moment and soak in the glory of the scene, thanking God for being the Master Gardener.

When thinking about designing your outdoor space, consider the following items as a helpful checklist:

1. Natural Elements

These are existing or introduced components from the natural environment:

- Topography – shape and contour of the land (hills, slopes, grading)
- Vegetation – trees, shrubs, ground cover, and lawns
- Water Features – ponds, streams, fountains, rain gardens
- Soil – type, quality, and drainage capabilities
- Climate and microclimate – sun, wind, and rainfall patterns

2. Built Elements (Hardscape)

Constructed components that provide structure, function, and access:

- Paths and walkways – concrete, gravel, pavers, stepping stones
- Patios, decks, and terraces – outdoor gathering areas
- Walls and fences – for privacy, retention, or aesthetics
- Structures – pergolas, gazebos, benches, lighting, signage
- Drainage and irrigation systems – to manage water flow and plant health

3. Planting Design (Softscape)

Focuses on the composition and purpose of plant materials:

- Plant selection – based on climate, aesthetics, maintenance, and use
- Color and texture – seasonal variation, contrast, and harmony
- Scale and form – matching plant size and shape to site conditions
- Function – shade, screening, habitat, erosion control

4. Functional Considerations

Addresses how people interact with the space:

- Circulation – movement through the site (pedestrian and vehicular)
- Accessibility – is there someone in your family that needs mobility accommodations? Should the space be kid-friendly?
- Safety and visibility – lighting, sightlines, and secure environments
- Zoning – defining space for recreation, relaxation, work, or utility

5. Aesthetic and Cultural Aspects

Design choices that shape mood, meaning, and visual appeal:

- Focal points and viewsheds – creating interest and framing views
- Symmetry vs. asymmetry – balance and visual rhythm
- Cultural and historical references – integrating heritage or symbolism (think the American flag, the Texas star, Talavera pottery, Pagodas, etc.)
- Thematic design – such as formal gardens, native landscapes, or minimalist settings

6. Environmental Sustainability

Integration of eco-friendly (not to mention wallet-friendly) and regenerative practices:

- Stormwater management – bioswales, permeable surfaces, rain gardens
- Native and drought-tolerant plants – reduce water use and support ecosystems
- Soil health and composting – promote long-term viability
- Green infrastructure – living walls, green roofs, carbon offsetting

Gardening isn't just for the green thumbs or weekend warriors. You can also include your little ones in the gardening process. Nowadays you can find children's size gloves, shovels and aprons at many retailers. I find that kiddos make the cutest gardeners on earth, and they really enjoy "helping" mama in the yard. My little one started out at about eighteen months old by touting her new walking prowess and transferring small rocks from one location of the yard to another. Instead of growing frustrated by her "making a mess" on her fruitless mission, I'd pause, take some deep belly breaths (these are a life saver to me, they regulate your Central Nervous System free of charge!) and say softly, "Thank you Lord for Stella Grace". Then by two years old, she was able to do all of the container garden watering for me!

Chapter 2
Home & Garage Organization

"For God is not a God of disorder but of peace - as in all the congregations of the Lord's people." 1 Corinthians 14:33

I'm not sure where the saying "cleanliness is next to Godliness" came from, but I think they were on to something. There is something so pure and so gratifying about a clean and organized home. Our God is a God of order, structure, peace, taxonomy even. Having my home clean, neat and tidy, and organized gives me a tremendous sense of peace and satisfaction, and the converse is true. I get anxious if I see a lot of visual clutter, chaos, crumbs, etc., then I find myself feeling irritable and losing my patience in my heart with my family instead of pausing to take some deep breaths, drink some water, and ask for their help in dealing with the household situation.

When it comes to personal or professional organization, I pride myself on my filing systems, goals, to do lists, and productivity. I am admittedly a dopamine junkie when it comes to crossing things off my list. The only way I can function is to keep a dynamic to do list. I know of and respect so many methods out there, apps, journals, etc., but for me, my command central lives in my To Dos note in my notes app on my iPhone. I live and breathe by it. I also must admit that I am so driven by productivity that sometimes I catch myself (or the Holy Spirit nudges me) to surrender the list to the Lord. Anything we love more than God becomes an idol and I have to check myself on this front frequently.

In terms of home and physical organization, have some rules when it comes to home storage and organization. I hope they help you as much as they've helped me and my family:

1. A place for everything, and everything in its place.
2. Don't put it down, put it away.
3. Touch it once.
4. Invest in a label maker, this helps communicate to your family where things belong so they can help you put things away.
5. If something comes in, something goes out (this applies in particular to clothing and kids' toys).
6. Build up, utilize vertical real estate to get the most out of your cupboards and closets.

The Family Room

Is it me, or does it often seem like our children live in the house more than we do given their treasure trove of toys that once was a family room? It's a complete marvel to me how children seem to autonomously suck toys into their orbit with a remarkable gravitational force. That being said, I live by the creed that their toys belong in their rooms. A girlfriend with children older than mine shared that motto with me once, and it stayed with me until I had children of my own. Family spaces are communal, and in our household, to be shared, having respect for the people you share it with (think cups laying around, cereal bowls left on the coffee table, candy wrappers on the rug). Chaos. It's a no-no at Casa de Romero. By the same token, we don't live with toys strewn all over the family room. Obviously, it happens of course, but that's why I've enacted the "nightly refresh." This is where I essentially apply the same rule about coming home to a clean house after a vacation (and therefore picking it up before we leave) to going to bed at night. I don't want to wake up to visual clutter of any kind, so we pick up after ourselves before we go to bed at night. I take pride in teaching my son in particular that picking up the floor of his room and making his bed every morning contributes to his mental health. Raising him with an emphasis on and value assigned to things being neat and tidy in his living space is something I am very proud of.

That same girlfriend taught me something I can only refer to as a life hack because it's so genius. She would attach a short note to her children's birthday party invitations that said *no gifts, please*, but she'd offer that guests could give a modest contribution to their college fund. Genius. For years I have included the same sentiment in my children's party invitations, *"AJ has all the presents he needs, your presence is a present indeed, but if you feel so inclined to give a gift, please consider a small contribution to his college fund."* At best, your kid walks away with a ton of cash that you can deposit into their account (it is very simple to set up either a proper college fund or a savings account for your child that is earmarked for their future education). At worst, some kind soul still brings a present for your child. Win-win. Either way, your house isn't becoming overrun with toys at every possible holiday and life celebration.

Another note on children's toys is that if you've run out of space, it's time to donate. I know it can be challenging, but doing so has a number of benefits, including the fact that you can involve your children in the donation process and let them know that their old toys are going to bless another child, and very likely a child in need.

The Kitchen

Over the years, I've researched, been taught, and personally implemented a variety of kitchen organization strategies that have truly transformed how I use and enjoy the space in my kitchen. My Aunt Mary Jane is an organizational whiz and has taught me a lot about using space to your advantage. From grouping items by function to creating efficient work zones, small but intentional implementations make a big difference in both flow and functionality. I've discovered the value of clear containers, vertical storage, and regular decluttering- each one a simple habit that helps maintain order in a busy kitchen. In this list, I'm sharing seven of my favorite tips that have stood the test of time and can make every day cooking feel a little more seamless and satisfying.

1. Group Kitchen Goods by Function
Organize items based on how and where you use them:

- Keep cutting boards near prep surfaces.
- Store pots and pans near the stove.
- Place coffee supplies together near the machine.

2. Use Zones
Create work "zones" such as:

- Prep zone – knives, mixing bowls, measuring tools.
- Cooking zone – spatulas, pots, oils, spices.
- Baking zone- cake pans, pie plates, flour sifter, sieves, etc.
- Cleaning zone – dish soap, towels, scrubbers.
- Storage zone – foil, containers, plastic wrap, Ziplock baggies, etc.

3. Declutter Regularly
- Purge expired items, duplicate gadgets, and tools you never use. Keep only what you truly need and use. Donate anything else.

4. Maximize Vertical Space
   - The key to good organization is utilizing your vertical real estate. Use risers whenever you can to create a shelf within a shelf so items can be placed on top of others. Use the tops of cabinets for seasonal or lesser-used items such as soup tureen or even pitchers. Use stackable bins to make it tidy and safe. Use shelf risers, wall hooks, or magnetic strips for knives. Consider hanging mugs or utensils under cabinets.

5. Clear the Countertops
   - Only keep daily-use items out (e.g., toaster, fruit bowl). Store the rest to reduce visual clutter and create more prep space.

6. Use Clear Containers
   - Decant dry goods like pasta, rice, and flour into clear containers for visibility and to preserve freshness. Label them for easy access.

7. Lazy Susans & Drawer Dividers
   - Use lazy Susans in corner cabinets or the fridge.
   - Install drawer organizers for utensils, gadgets, and spices.

Bedroom Closets

As I mentioned, a tried-and-true rule we live by in my house is: something in, something out. This most aptly applies to bedroom closets and clothing. If we come home with new back to school clothes, or the kids are given new wardrobes by the grandparents for Christmas (bless them), we purge. If you don't have unlimited storage or a walk-in closet (like me) or even if you do, but just never seem to have enough space, consider storing your seasonal clothes, labeled, in clear plastic bins under your bed. No space under there? Put your bed on six-inch risers, and you'll gain valuable extra storage space. I rotate my husband's and my clothes only twice a year: for spring and summer, and for fall and winter. Things that get stored seasonally for me are things like bathing suits and cover ups, scarves and winter coats, wool sweaters and the like. Things I store for my husband are his Hawaiian shirts and seasonal buttons ups, and thick heavy jackets (yes, we live in Southern California, but he runs cold and we do drive to the mountains every year to experience the snow with the kids and the grandparents). This project isn't very time consuming and often I even keep things on their hangers and just fold them into the bins (my mom actually does this with her suitcases when she travels!).

As our life has gotten fuller and busier and there's just no bandwidth for me to engage in every household project on my own, I will ask my husband for about ten minutes of his time on the weekend, which he's happy to do, to help pull out the bins from under the bed and hand me clothes to switch out, then he puts them back under the bed for me. Easy peasy, lemon squeezy.

Donations. Not to get all corporate on you, but running your home is like running a business. You are the CEO and the CPHG (Chief Purveyor of Household Goods). That means you're basically running an import / export business. Things come in, things need to go out. Enter the all magical donations box (ooooh, ahhh). I cannot recommend highly enough having a central repository for things you and your family no longer use, and most importantly, *know* that you'll no longer use. I keep ours in the garage and yes, I'm the only one who makes deposits, but my family knows its there, and what my system is, so I'm calling that a win.

Things that go in our donation box are; household appliances we no longer use because maybe we've upgraded or simply don't use them at all, clothing, plushies, toys, and anything else we no longer have a need for. When I first got married I geeked out on creating my wedding registry, fulfilling all my wildest dreams; rice cookers, poached egg contraptions, etc, only to find that I prefer the old fashioned way of cooking most things, like rice and eggs. Not to mention, I had to be strategic with my use of space in the kitchen. I've found that I prefer to give real estate to my vases, glassware, and hosting accessories, over things that don't bring my heart joy. I'll never forget the day when I finally pulled the plug (ha) on my convection oven. It had sat on my kitchen counter for years, and we only turned to it once or twice a year for particular things. To be honest it was kind of painful to let it go, but I had to be realistic that I wasn't using it and much preferred the ease and versatility of my air fryer. So off it went to be loved by some other family, and in its place, I was able to stylize my cookbooks.

Hall Closets

Here are some practical tips and tricks for keeping hall closets organized, whether they're used for coats, linens, cleaning supplies, or catch-all storage. If your home doesn't have hall closets, there are other options you can use such as in-bathroom storage solutions to keep your towels and linens stocked.

1. Define the Closet's Purpose
   - Decide what the hall closet is for- coats, towels, tools, or multipurpose- and stick to that focus to prevent clutter creep.

2. Use Clear Bins and Labels
   - Store smaller items (light bulbs, batteries, medicines, extra toiletries) in clear, labeled bins so you can see what's inside at-a-glance.

3. Add Baskets or Drawers for Loose Items
   - Use baskets or pull-out drawers for gloves, scarves, or reusable bags. It keeps shelves tidy and makes grabbing essentials quick.

4. Install Door Organizers
   - Use over-the-door racks or hanging organizers for small items like umbrellas, cleaning bottles, or shoes to maximize vertical space.

5. Rotate Seasonally
   - Switch out items based on the season- store winter gear higher up in summer and move pool towels or sandals to the back in winter. Doing this proactively will save you a lot of headache when the time comes that you're rushing out the door with the kids and you need your seasonal items pronto.

6. Use Shelf Risers or Stackable Bins
   - Double your space by adding risers or using stackable bins for items like linens or paper goods.

7. Hang a Pegboard or Hooks Inside the Door
   - Perfect for hanging dustpans, keys, or pet leashes- utilize every inch of space, especially on the insides of your doors.

8. Do a Quarterly (or more often) Clean-Out
   - Make it a habit to declutter every few months- toss expired items, donate unused gear, and realign items with your closet's purpose.

The Garage

Keeping a garage organized takes a bit of strategy, but with a few smart systems, you can maximize space and actually find what you need when you need it. And if you don't have a garage, these ideas can still be applied in carports or modified for use in apartment parking that comes with storage.

Here are some practical ideas:

1. Go Vertical
   - Use wall space for shelves, pegboards, and hooks. Hang tools, bikes, ladders, and garden gear to free up the floor.
2. Use Clear Bins and Labels
   - Store seasonal items, holiday decor, or sports gear in clear plastic bins with bold labels. Group similar items together for easy access.
3. Install Overhead Storage
   - Ceiling-mounted racks are great for long-term storage (like camping gear or bins you only need a few times a year).
4. Create Zones
   - Divide the garage into functional zones- tools, yardwork, car care, sports equipment, and storage. This helps everyone know where things belong.
5. Use a Workbench or Rolling Tool Chest
   - Designate a workspace for repairs or DIY projects and keep tools organized in drawers or magnetic strips.
6. Keep Your Donation Bin Handy
   - Once you've tossed all unused or outgrown items into your bin and it's full, donate. This prevents clutter from building up.
7. Maximize Corners
   - Install corner shelving or use stackable bins to take advantage of often wasted space.
8. Leave Room for the Cars
   - Make sure whatever system you install still allows car doors to open comfortably. Outline parking zones with tape if necessary.

Chapter 3
Interior Design & Décor

"But as for me and my house, we will serve the Lord." Joshua 24:15

Design and decoration have been a passion in both theory and practice for me my whole life, and I wanted to share what I've learned with you. Additionally, as I write this we are breaking ground on a room addition at my home that will feature a family room, and a formal dining room and I am thoroughly enjoying the process of developing and articulating my ideas, sourcing windows, sofas and fabrics, and selecting my aesthetic style. There are a number of different programs that you can use to both layout the blueprint of your space, and to design the interior. For designing I use a hybrid technique which also includes hand drawings. I am not an artist by any stretch of the imagination, my husband is the artist, but I find it useful to scratch out a framework of a plan as a jumping off point. It also advises me in creating my shopping list, so I know exactly what I need to purchase. I have a handful of home décor stores I love to shop with and know that no matter what time of year it may be, there will be great options and beautiful finds. Some of those stores are Hobby Lobby (they're Christian-owned too and play worship music in their store, which warms my heart), Traditions, Aldik Home, Winward Home, Designer's Studio, and Home Goods.

A Guide to Beautiful, Functional Spaces

There's a beautiful joy in walking into a space that feels just right. The colors please the eyes, the furniture flows, and there's a sense of calm and order. You may not be able to name exactly what makes it work- but you feel it. That's the power of interior design. Interior design isn't about chasing trends or copying magazine spreads. It's about creating spaces that serve your family well, reflect your personal style, and support the way you want to live. Hospitality is a spiritual gift and matters greatly to the Kingdom. Whether you're decorating a small apartment, refreshing a tired room, or setting up your dream home, a little design knowledge goes a long way. Great design doesn't happen by accident; there are hidden rules behind every beautiful room. Great interior design is built on a few guiding principles that help create balance, flow, and harmony in your space.

Here are some of the basics- what I call *Interior Design 101*- to help you approach your home with confidence, creativity, and care.

1. Balance

Balance is about distributing visual weight evenly.

- Symmetrical balance creates a mirror image- think matching chairs on either side of a fireplace.
- Asymmetrical balance feels more relaxed, using different elements with equal weight.
- Radial balance radiates around a center point, like chairs surrounding a round table.

2. Rhythm

- Rhythm guides the eye. You can create rhythm by repeating shapes, colors, or patterns throughout a room, or by gradually changing an element (such as candleholders in ascending height).

3. Emphasis

- Every room needs a focal point- a fireplace, a piece of art, or a statement light fixture. This "anchor" draws the eye and grounds the space.

4. Proportion and Scale

- Choose pieces that are the right size for the room and each other. A tiny rug under a giant sofa will always feel off. A well-scaled space feels just right.

5. Harmony and Unity

- These principles bring everything together. They help different elements- colors, textures, styles- feel like they belong in the same story.

There are also elements of design to consider. Think of the following as the ingredients in your design recipe. When used thoughtfully, they elevate even the simplest room.

Welcome Home: *A Guide to Homemaking, From the Heart*

Color

- Color sets the mood.
- Warm colors (reds, yellows, oranges) feel cozy and energizing.
- Cool colors (blues, greens, grays) create calm and spaciousness.
- Use the color wheel to build harmonious palettes or add contrast for interest.

Texture

- Layering smooth and rough textures adds depth. Combine wood, linen, glass, and metal to make a space feel rich and lived-in.

Light

- Lighting affects how everything else looks.
- Ambient lighting is general (ceiling lights).
- Task lighting is for specific activities (reading lamps).
- Accent lighting highlights special features (wall sconces, picture lights).
- Natural light is always a bonus- use it well!

Use of Space

Design is as much about what you *don't* fill as what you do. Leave breathing room around furniture. Negative space is your friend.

Line

Lines influence how your space feels.
Horizontal lines create calm and stability.
Vertical lines add energy and height.
Curved or diagonal lines bring softness and movement.

Form

Form refers to the shape of things. Geometric forms (squares, rectangles) feel modern and structured. Organic forms (curves, natural shapes) feel relaxed and welcoming.

You don't need a degree to design a beautiful space (although working with a professional can be invaluable), just a thoughtful approach. I am very blessed to have gotten to work with my Aunt Janice Herr, a professional interior designer. Projects we've worked on together have ranged from apartments, to offices, to full homes. Here are a few step-by-step guidelines for the process of designing a space.

1. Define the Purpose
   - Determine how a room will be used and by Whom (i.e., a family-friendly living room which needs comfort and durability, or a serene office that needs clarity and function).

2. Gather Inspiration
   - Start a Pinterest board or clip magazine photos. You'll start to see patterns in what you love- perhaps light colors, rustic touches, clean lines, etc. This will help you clarify your style.

3. Set a Budget
   - Decide what you can spend, then prioritize. Sometimes all a space needs is paint, pillows, and rearranged furniture, but planning helps you gain focus and rein you in when your creative juices are flowing and you feel you've just got to have…everything.

4. Create a Floor Plan
   - Measure the room. Sketch out a layout. Free online tools like Roomstyler or graph paper and a ruler will do just fine to help you get your thoughts organized before you start buying or moving anything.

5. Choose a Color Scheme and Materials
   - Pick a palette (neutrals + 1-2 accent colors). Choose durable finishes, especially in high-traffic areas while considering aesthetic appeal. Mix soft and hard textures for balance.

6. Add Furniture and Decor in Layers
   - Start with larger items (sofa, bed), then layer in rugs, curtains, lighting, and accessories. Add personality through artwork, plants, pillows, books, family photos, flowers, and collected treasures.

A Quick Tour of Popular Styles

You don't need to fit into a box, but knowing some common styles can help you define your taste.
- Traditional – Classic furniture, rich wood tones, symmetry, and historical influences.
- Modern – Clean lines, minimal clutter, neutral palettes, and functional design.
- Farmhouse – Rustic textures, neutrals, natural materials, shiplap, and cozy charm.
- Bohemian – Eclectic, layered, full of color, pattern, and personality.
- Scandinavian – Minimalist, bright, and functional with soft textures and light woods.
- Transitional – A blend of traditional warmth and modern simplicity.
- Eclectic – A curated blend of diverse design elements- mixing eras, textures, and influences- to create a cohesive and deeply personal space.

A Word on the Eclectic Style

My style is and has always been eclectic. I used to feel bad about this, thinking that I "should" have a style that's more comprehensive. But from an interior design perspective, the eclectic style is whole and complete. It is expressed by its intentional mix of elements from different time periods, styles, textures, and colors- all curated in a way that feels harmonious, expressive, and very personal.

It's not random or chaotic- it's *layered*. While eclectic interiors often include a variety of design influences (mid-century modern paired with boho, or traditional furniture alongside modern art), they are thoughtfully pulled together through cohesive elements like:

- A unifying color palette
- Repeating textures or shapes
- Balanced visual weight
- Curated collections and meaningful pieces

The eclectic style allows for freedom and creativity. It's ideal for those who want their home to reflect their stories, travels, interests, and contradictions- all in one space. It celebrates both contrast and connection. In short, the eclectic design is the artful blend of the unexpected- where contrast meets cohesion, and personal expression takes center stage.

In closing, interior design is about creating a space that serves you and blesses those who walk through your door. A thoughtfully designed home supports your routines, reflects your values, and makes room for connection and rest. So don't stress about perfection. Design is a journey- one that grows as you do. The more you trust your instincts and build your home with love and purpose, the more beautiful it will feel, and the more blessings it will have to bestow.

Chapter 4
Cleaning & Care

"Finally, brothers and sisters, whatever is true, whatever is noble, whatever is right, whatever is pure, whatever is lovely, whatever is admirable- if anything is excellent or praiseworthy- think about such things. Whatever you have learned or received, or heard from me, or seen in me- put it into practice. And the God of peace will be with you."
Philippians 4:8-9

I have a confession to make. I did not learn how to clean until I was married and had children. It's not that I had a dirty (never) or untidy (God forbid) home before, it's just that the reality of needing to get down and dirty with some gnarly messes never occurred until I lived with a husband, children, and pets. I went straight from school into the workforce as a teenager and was never afforded the luxury (and yes, a clean home is a luxury because so many of us know that life has a tendency to take over even the best laid intentions to pick up things and wipe down surfaces) to learn how to properly clean anything more than the dishes I ate dinner on.

Additionally, a generational woe I've encountered is the replaceability of things. My Nana knew how to clean anything, because she was born during the great depression and you made what you had last forever. By the 1990s goods became utterly disposable as the revolutions in industries made it easier than ever to buy and throw away.

Nevertheless, cleaning is an art and a science, and I respect both. That being said, you would be blown away to learn how many things just lemons, baking soda, and white vinegar can clean and cure, but no matter how simple it may be, like most of us, I just don't have a lot of time to clean during the week. So, I have a few strategies that serve me well to combat my lack of time and real need to clean. The first is that years ago, I invested in a Roomba. They're not terribly expensive, and the peace of mind it gives you is priceless. When I am short on time and seeing small messes all around the house on the floor (stray Cheerios, leaves, shredded bits of toilet paper, you name it), with a push of a button, I'm able to tackle it and be doing something else I consider to be a more important use of my time, like supervising my son's homework, listening to my husband talk about his day at work, making dinner, or coloring with my daughter.

I also have dust busters or handheld vacuums squirreled away all over the place. I have one in each bathroom, one under the kitchen sink, one in the garage, and one in the car. These are inexpensive gadgets that buy me a tremendous amount of sanity, because I can tackle a mess in real time and without a lot of fuss. I have both electric charging and battery-operated ones, and I'm impartial to either. What's important to me is that I know I have the tools where I need them for easy cleanup.

Another resource I rely heavily on and buy multiples of is lint rollers. I swear animal fur is part sticky because it shows up everywhere, so I keep a lint roller in the magazine rack by the couch, in my bathroom, in my closet, and in my car. This way, I can quickly spruce up my clothing and don't have to go rummaging around or to another location to feel clean.

I also enlist my family in adopting daily habits or rules of the house that help contribute to a cleaner home:

1. Taking off shoes at the front door. Whether you use a basket, an entryway table, a small shoe shelf or bench, get those shoes off before walking around in your home. Think of all the germs, bacteria, and simply general dust and dirt that we walk around on out there. Bringing that inside of your home and onto your floors? Eeeew, no thank you.

2. Maintaining clean tools and instruments. Washing machines need to be cleaned, sponges need to be sanitized, and vacuum bags need to be emptied. Taking the time to wash your washing machine with one cycle or microwave your sponge for 30 seconds to kill off any germs or

empty your vacuum bag can not only keep your house easily cleaned, but it's also satisfying. You can wash your dishwasher with a simple solution of distilled white vinegar and baking soda. Need to sanitize your children's hard plastic toys? Let your dishwasher do that work for you!

3. Clearing paper clutter. Bills go to a designated location where you pay them, children's crafts and report cards go into memorabilia albums, on the fridge, or get tossed. Junk mail immediately goes into the trash. Items you need to file go into a filing folder for sorting when you have a moment to handle that task. A place for everything, and everything in its place. Even for paper too.

4. Purge food from the fridge. I talk a lot about preventing food waste later on in this book, but for now, just know that dealing with your fridge is an almost daily task when you have a family, to ensure that you have only what your family will eat and that food is stored safely.

5. Making beds daily. I have raised my children with the idea that making their beds and picking up their rooms contributes to good mental health. Having an untidy bedroom floor or an unmade bed looks and feels uninviting, stressful, and even a little depressing. When beds are made and floors are cleared daily for a nice reset, we can bloom where we are planted and have our personal spaces ready to host us and make us feel happy to be in them.

6. Dirty dishes never stay in the sink. It's true that throughout the course of a single day or even meal, your kitchen sink can pile up and your cup overflow… with dishes, however, don't go to bed leaving dirty dishes in the sink. Not only is it unsanitary, but it can invite unwanted pests, or even your own pets, into inappropriate places of your home. In a similar way, limit where food is eaten in your home. Food should be consumed in designated areas only and picked up immediately once done. Additionally, your dishes, sponges, sink and countertops will remain more consistently clean and need less intervention if everything is at least made clean and put right before going to bed. (If you ever visit my home, you're more than likely to be greeted by some dishes in the drying rack, but hey, at least they're clean and shiny.)

7. Use multiple cleaning wipes for different surfaces. No one wants to transfer bacteria from one location to another while cleaning, but unless your wipes have enough moisture to keep the surface area wet for at least a minute, you're not properly sanitizing. So, break out a few to several wipes to get the job done well.

8. Wet towels or shower curtains should be hung out flat for drying. No bunching of the shower curtain especially while wet, or God forbid a wet towel on the floor. These need to air dry with as much surface area exposed as possible, so they must get hung up properly. Towels will need washing less often this way too. (Less laundry, yay!)

9. Do a little every day. Clean as you go, reset every night, pick up in whatever room you're in. However, you want to teach your family to care for the home, I'm here for it. The alternative is living in a constant state of clutter (how upsetting) and then being overwhelmed at the prospect of cleaning it all up. (And mind you, tidying up a space is a precursor to actually cleaning it, so let's not play double-jeopardy and ensure we're maintaining what I call "organized chaos" and nightly resets.)

The Methodology

The old-fashioned concept of using elbow grease is not lost on me, at the same time though, I have multiple priorities pawing at me every single day, often at the same time, so working smarter not harder is my motto. My methodology for cleaning is to let the appliances work for me. When I have thirty minutes and it's "go time" to clean, I get the dishwasher, the washing machine, and the Roomba going. I also allow cleaning products their time required to take effect. You may be surprised to know that if you read the back of most bathroom tile and shower cleaners, the manufacturer recommends allowing the product to sit for several minutes on the surface area before you begin to scrub. Doing so allows the cleanser to work for you, so you can get a few more things done, such as tidying up toys, blankets, and other things around your house that are on a field trip from their proper home. Cleaning experts will tell you to pick a room and stick with it. At my house I have found that picking a task and sticking with it is much more effective. If I'm picking up things, I'm doing that across the house. If I'm doing laundry, everyone's clothes are being handled, if I'm dealing with dishes, they're all getting washed, and put away immediately (if I'm lucky), along with countertops being wiped down or sanitized with Clorox wipes, depending on their need. (I am a big fan of Clorox wipes.) I'm in my mama era, so while I'd love to be as sustainable as possible in everything I do, while my kids are little, I have to do what I can when I can. For me, that looks like quick, effective cleansing wipes and not the more traditional method of spray and a rag that then needs to be washed. Play to your family's strengths and preferences. I like washing the dishes, I totally don't mind it. There's something so satisfying about taking something dirty and fixing it up. Vacuuming on the other hand? Not a fan. Ask your family members what chores they would like to participate in and then ask them to complete them when they need doing. I do not expect my family to anticipate or even see needs around the house. Maybe my expectations are too low, maybe they're a hot mess. Either way. What works for my family is that we all have our chore preferences, so when I ask, I usually get agreeableness and immediate action. Yay!

The last thing I'll say about methodology is to watch the clock or set a timer when you clean. I'm a super-duper clock watcher, so I'll buzz around and get my tasks handled in my allotted time whether that's 15 minutes or 30 minutes. Either way, I have defined a start and end time for my tasks, and I've found that that's motivational for me, so I don't stall and just do the darn thing.

I also apply this method at the gym. In years gone by, I could spend over an hour doing all the things I wanted to accomplish at the gym. Nowadays I don't have that kind of time. So my perfect workout is a hard hitting thirty minutes. That's all I need to run and get my cardio in or complete strength training. When I know I only have half an hour, I get after it with a sense of purpose and urgency and move on with my day.

Here are some tidbits I've learned as I've focused on becoming "good" at cleaning.

1. To clean copper-bottom pots, use ketchup.
2. To clear a clogged drain, pour ½ cup salt, ½ cup baking soda, and ¼ cup of vinegar down the drain. Plug drain until the fizzing stops, then flush with boiling water.
3. To remove ink stains from carpet, soak the stained area with lemon juice, scrub, and rinse with water.
4. To remove mud or soot from rugs or carpet, sprinkle salt on the stained area. Allow the salt to dry or settle for 10-15 minutes, then vacuum.
5. To make a microwave smell fresh and to loosen hardened food splatter (if you don't have a microwave food guard, I highly recommend one!), fill a microwave safe cup with water and 1 tablespoon of lemon juice. Heat the water at full power for one minute.
6. To sanitize sponges that have started to smell, microwave for thirty seconds.
7. To remove crayon marks from painted walls, scrub with a dab of non-gel toothpaste.
8. To remove gum from clothing, freeze it with a piece of ice. Then the hardened gum can be crumbled and brushed off.

Laundry

Washing laundry is simple enough, but when it comes to kids and their messes and stains, that is another subject. When tackling tough stains, whether by hand or in the machine, always use hot water. Hot water opens up the fabric weave of the garment so your stain fighter or soap can penetrate and lift out the stains. I usually hand wash crazy stains in my kitchen sink where I can employ my tea kettle to give me piping hot water, and I use OxiClean with a toothbrush to scrub away even the gnarliest stains.

Equip your laundry area with all the essentials you may need to handle everything at the same time and in the same place; detergent of course, stain pre-treaters, a stain remover brush such as an old toothbrush, a small wash tub for delicates or general handwashing, a drying rack and a steamer for wrinkles.

To clean your clothes washer, simply add 1 quart of bleach to the empty washer and run a hot water cycle, with an extra rinse cycle. Alternatively, you could use four cups of white vinegar on hot for the longest wash cycle.

If you're anything like me, you'll run out of laundry detergent once or twice. Let me guess, someone used the last of the laundry detergent and not only did they not put it on the shopping list, but they didn't even tell you, right? Now, with your hydrating facemask on, your hair in curlers, your load in the washer, and the goal you thought you had for getting three things done in the five minutes before your coffee finally ices over like a winter pond is gone because you have no laundry detergent. It's ok mama. Take three deep breaths and head to your pantry, add one cup of baking soda or borax to the load, then run it as usual. (Baking soda helps to regulate the pH level of water in the washer, striking the perfect balance between alkaline and acidity, which also helps eliminate bacteria.)

Now for your dryer. Did you know that excess lint in a dryer's vent system is a leading cause of house fires? Keep your dryer as free from lint as possible after every use. I have found that picking lint from the drum is something my toddler loves to do with her little fingers. And guess what? You can actually use your dryer lint in your compost bin because it's composed of cotton! I love to air dry laundry, but only in the summer, when the temperatures almost mirror that of the inside of the dryer. It saves money on electricity, is good for the environment, and gives me a chance to thank God for the truly awesome power of sunlight.

Cleaning by Room

Just like other household projects (gardening, sewing, etc.), cleaning requires gear. I recommend storing caddies underneath each sink in your house, and keeping them stocked with the essentials, which takes away a huge hurdle to the cleaning process by having everything you need readily available as you try to do the darn thing.

All-purpose items you should have in each caddy are; microfiber cloths, cotton cloths, paper towels, spray bottles, glass cleaner, a scrub brush, magic eraser, dish soap (a good quality kind such as Dawn), cleaning vinegar, baking soda, duster, and gloves. Now let's tackle this concept by area.

The Kitchen

Interestingly enough, you can clean a lot of your kitchen with what you likely already have in your kitchen.

- Ketchup can be used to bring copper pots and pans back to life, cutting through grime and shining at the same time. The acetic acid is the secret ingredient, it resolves tarnish and leaves your pots and pans looking great.

- Distilled white vinegar can help remove baked-on stains stemming from BBQ sauce, ketchup, spaghetti sauce, and many other types of goop.

- Lemons work as an awesome polish for dull stainless-steel pans. They're a natural brightener! All you have to do is cut a lemon in half and use it on the pan as you would a sponge.

Caring for sterling silver doesn't have to be a pain. I have some amazing pieces I've thrifted or inherited from my Nana and Great Aunt that I use at every opportunity. Silver is just so classy and timeless. I like Wright's Silver Cream for polishing my sterling silver. There are some solutions that include aluminum foil and hot water, but I like my polish.

My Aunt Mary Jane gave me a wonderful homemade solution to Windex, no offense to Windex, or the dad in *My Big Fat Greek Wedding*. It's more economical and has way less chemicals. To create your own glass cleaner, mix together 1 ½ cups water, 1 ½ Tablespoons rubbing alcohol, and 1 ½ Tablespoons vinegar. This will leave your glassware, which can dull down from hard water deposits, looking sparkly and gorgeous. This also works of course on your windows and can also be used on other surfaces such as tile and chrome.

To clean your (stainless steel) sink, sprinkle the sink with baking soda. Baking soda cuts through grease and will remove food particles. Lightly scrub the sink to work it in. Then spray it with distilled white vinegar. The acidity in the vinegar will cut through mineral deposits that cause spots and streaks. Once the fizzing stops, rinse with warm water, and you're done! To clean the top of your stove, countertops, appliances, and floor you can use equal parts vinegar and water.

*Note: if you're not a fan of the smell of vinegar, you can enhance it using some essential oils you very well may already have on hand. Awesome scents you can employ for this use are; eucalyptus, mint, lime grapefruit, rosemary, lemon, lavender, and tea tree.

Let's talk about cleaning pots and pans next. It's kind of a joke at my house, I can burn water. The issue is that I am usually multi-tasking doing too many things (our strengths, when overdone, become weaknesses) and the next thing I know, I've created carbon. So, if you have a burned pan and would like to get rid of those scorch marks, fear not. The fix is simple. Using water and baking soda, make a thin paste and cover the scorch marks, working in the paste. Then rinse with boiling hot water. Wipe or scrub the pot to remove the burn marks. You can also add coarse salt to this method for extra stubborn stains. An alternative method, if you can believe it, is using a dryer sheet! (It's true what they say, truth really is stranger than fiction.) To use this method, just put a dryer sheet in a stained or scorched pot or pan with hot water. Let it sit for about an hour, then scrub away. (Thanks Martha Stewart!)

How to Clean Pans and Cookie Sheets

Nonstick frying pans- baking soda can be used to clean up your frying pans from strong smells and stains. Cover the bottom of the pan with a paste made from baking soda and water. Let the pan sit for a few hours. Then dilute the paste by adding more water to the pan. Bring the solution to a boil on the stovetop, then allow it to cool. Scrub, rinse, and you'll be off to the races!

Copper bottoms- my Nana taught me this trick when I was a young girl. To return copper bottomed pots and pans to their former glory, sprinkle baking soda all over the bottom of the pan (turned upside down). Then pour vinegar over the bottom of the pan. Cut a lemon in half and use it to scrub everywhere the copper should be brought out. Rinse the pot and dry thoroughly. Voilà!

Cookie sheets- sadly, cookie sheets are notorious for those little dark circles after just about one or two uses. To remove those stains and get pristine sheets again, mix baking soda with hydrogen peroxide from your medicine cabinet. Apply this solution to the cookie sheet and let it rest for about ninety minutes. Rinse away the dried paste, wiping down gently with a sponge or cloth. Good as new!

I could go all day about the various kitchen gadgetry that exists, but for now, I'll just stick to some of the ones that get the dirtiest at my house.

The Fridge

As a rule of thumb, you should clean your fridge once a quarter. Take a look at the dates on condiments and toss anything that's past its expiration date. With a cloth or sponge and hot soapy water, you can tackle any mess easily inside your fridge. Add an opened box of baking soda to help absorb odors once you're done.

Garbage Disposal

I have a love-hate relationship with my garbage disposal, but be that as it may, I have to clean it periodically. Create a cleanser by pouring ½ cup baking soda into the disposal, followed by ½ cup of distilled white vinegar. This mixture will foam up, so have your drain stopper handy to plug the drain and keep all that cleaning foam inside. Once the fizzing stops, flush with hot water from the tap. If you have dual sinks, do this with both sides for the best results.

Microwave

Fill a bowl with one cup of water and add some lemon slices if you have them handy. Microwave the water for five minutes. Let it sit with the door closed, steaming for five more minutes. Then take a cloth and wipe down the inside with ease. Once you're done you can toss the rinds down the garbage disposal with some water and a few seconds of running to eliminate odors.

Substitution for Dishwasher Detergent

Fill the detergent cup with baking soda and run a cycle. Or fill a bowl with distilled white vinegar and place it in the top rack of the dishwasher, then run your cycle as normal. The force of the water will dole out the vinegar to clean your dishes for you.

Black Tea for Hardwood

This doesn't describe me with respect to my hardwood floors, but if you're an organic naturalist, did you know you can use black tea to clean your hardwood floors? True story. And they've been doing it for centuries. The astringency of tea cuts through grease, grime and dust like a hot knife through butter, and as an added bonus, it will add a shine to the floor. All you need to do is boil a pot of water with 5-7 tea bags depending on the surface area you'll be cleaning. Allow the tea to steep for about ten minutes, then add some ice cubes or cool water to lower the temperature, pour the tea into your mop bucket and have at it. Please note that this method only works on real wood, do not use this on laminate wood flooring.

A final note about kitchen cleaning is that if you have high cupboards like many of us do, a low profile, folding stepstool is a must so you can safely and easily get to the things you need.

Family Room

Having a clean family room starts with a clean vacuum. Keep your vacuum clean and ready when you are by regularly dumping out its bin and cleaning its filter. A vacuum will lose its suction power and effectiveness if its filter is full, or if the beater bars are tangled up with hair or string. With vacuums I think of the old adage, an ounce of prevention is worth a pound of cure. No one wants to take their time to clean these features out on their vacuum, but we both know you really don't want to spend your time doing this when the oven timer is sounding, your toddler just spilled kinetic sand all over the floor, and your phone is ringing. Come on. You can also use your vacuum cleaner to vacuum your fabric couches. I'm not sure how much my vacuum weighs, but I've had a bad back ever since an injury and a spine surgery in my 20s, yet I can lift my vacuum easily onto my couch to vacuum it, or use the attachment for this purpose. Did you know too that you can keep your upholstery and fabrics looking and smelling fabulous with just a box of baking soda and your vacuum? Just sprinkle the baking soda over your fabrics, work it in gently with the palm of your hand or a rag, let it sit for a few minutes to activate, then vacuum it up!

You may be surprised to know that you can make a natural furniture polish with just olive oil and lemons for your hardwood furniture. Mix one cup of olive oil with ½ cup of lemon juice to make an organic furniture polish.

Caring for leather (couches, chairs, decorative accents) is even easier than you might think. I've been really happy with the *Leather CPR* brand of leather cleaner. It's gentle enough for my leather handbags but tough enough for a couch or suitcase trunk. If you need to clean either aniline, semi-aniline, or pigmented leather, just vacuum away any crumbs or hair, wipe down with a clean cloth, and put together a mixture of a few drops of dish soap and warm water. Using a wet but wrung out cloth, work in small circles to clean the leather. Go over everything with a microfiber cloth to spiff up the leather afterward. Allow it to dry. There's no need to rinse it in any way.

Bathrooms

Keep your bathroom caddy stocked with a few essentials for easy, on-the-go cleaning. You can buy multipurpose cleaners or keep baking soda and vinegar in your caddy to use on the sink, tub, and shower tile. Also have on hand a nylon scrub brush, squeegee, cloths, and toilet bowl cleaner (you can also use undiluted vinegar for this is you prefer a more organic solution). Mixing household hydrogen peroxide and baking soda together into a thick paste makes for a fabulous grout cleaner. Lemons in the bathroom can also help dissolve hard water stains and soap scum due to the citric acid. It also serves as a non-abrasive, natural bleach to brighten things as you clean.

Clogged drains? If you don't want to use a harsh chemical like Drano, here's an organic recipe to unclog your drains. First pour boiling water into the drain, then pour ½ cup of baking soda followed by ½ cup of white vinegar into the drain. Wait about ten minutes, then pour more boiling hot water into the drain and flush with hot tap water for half a minute. Your drains will be good as new, no chemicals needed.

If you have rust stains, create a paste with baking soda and lemon juice to apply to the problem area. If you have hard water spots, distilled white vinegar is your best friend. The mild, acetic acid in it breaks the bonds that water minerals have formed. You could also use either lemon or lime juice instead, due to the citric acid.

Bedrooms

Teach your kids to make their beds. By the time they're in kindergarten, they can be helpful by learning to make their own bed. Until they become adept at it, you can opt to keep their bedding simple and do away with extra blankets. At this age children love to feel independent, capable, and successful, and making their bed is one way to accomplish this. This also allows them to arrange their plushies or pillows the way they'd like to. Remember for children, their plushies are like friends and they see them as personalities.

And if your creative little artists have gotten out of hand with crayons on a wooden surface, you can apply mayonnaise to the wood, rubbing it in until the crayon disappears. You can also enlist your little ones to help with this and even sing the clean up song together to make it fun.

Garage

If you don't have a garage, that's not a problem. Part of my proactive approach for keeping my house clean is the same concept I apply to the garage. That's the concept of "help me help you." I can have my house and spaces help me help them by having the right tools and materials located in the right locations. (The Lean Six Sigma Yellow Belt in me rejoices.) To this end, I keep a caddy of cleaning materials, as well as a shop vac, in my garage. At first, I wasn't into the shop vac, it was my husband's idea. But it really is an excellent cleaning solution in your garage, when you may have errant screws lying around or don't want to haul your interior vacuum cleaner into the garage.

No matter how you find what suits you when it comes to organizing your home, your family will take notice. They may never say anything, but as Proverbs 31 (aspiring) mamas, we can set the tone and maintain orderly, structured, beautiful homes. After all, our first ministry is within our very own homes.

Welcome Home: *A Guide to Homemaking From the Heart*

Chapter 5
Hosting

"Be joyful in hope, patient in affliction, faithful in prayer. Share with the Lord's people who are in need. Practice hospitality." Romans 12:12-13

Luk. 10, 38—42.

When it comes to the Biblical story of Mary and Martha, I am a Martha. While I have often gotten down on myself for this, accusing myself of being a "human doing" rather than a "human being," I'm reminded that in the Kingdom we all have a role to play, and until my day of perfect sanctification in the Lord, I find myself being most comfortable in actions- preparing, serving, cleaning up, and not in being still and unhurried. I've made strides in this area, but still, sitting down and enjoying a crossword puzzle or leafing through a magazine with a cup of herbal tea is a reward I only allow myself at the very end of the day. (Did I say day? It's usually dark out so we'll go with end of the night.) As I've gotten older, and as my marriage has matured, I have learned to communicate needs I see the household or the family has with my husband so he can help me, so I'm not collapsing at the end of each day, too worn out to even keep my eyes open.

As I've hosted throughout the years and applied myself to be a student of my craft, I've picked up a few things along the way I'd like to share with you. Just bear in mind that hosting doesn't have to be a stressful event. Hosting guests at home is as much about how people feel as it is about what you provide.

Here are some thoughtful tips to keep in mind for a warm, welcoming, and stress-free hosting experience:

1. Set the Tone at the Door
   - Greet guests personally and warmly. A tidy entryway, light music, and a pleasant scent (like a candle or fresh flowers) instantly create a welcoming atmosphere.

2. Prepare in Advance
   - Do as much as you can ahead of time- food prep, drink setup, cleaning- so you're present and relaxed when guests arrive.

3. Create Comfortable Spaces
   - Make sure there's enough seating and that it encourages conversation. Add cozy touches like throw blankets, soft lighting, or background music.

4. Offer a Drink Early On
   - Whether it's water, wine, or a signature mocktail, offering a beverage helps guests feel at ease and signals that they're being cared for.

5. Be Attentive, Not Overbearing
   - Circulate, chat, and notice if someone needs a refill or a new napkin- but also give people space to mingle and enjoy themselves naturally.

6. Be Mindful of Dietary Restrictions
   - Ask in advance if anyone has food allergies or dietary needs and offer at least one inclusive option that everyone can enjoy.

7. Tidy Restrooms & Essentials
   - Check that the bathroom is clean and stocked with fresh towels, hand soap, and toilet paper. A small vase of flowers or a candle is a nice touch. When I was a young girl, I discovered the craft of soap petals, and it made an impression on me that stuck. All you have to do is take artificial rose petals and dip them into melted soap, so that when they dry, you're left with a beautiful rose petal encased in soap, perfect for single use and provides a novel delight for your guests. Not to mention they look great in a glass bowl next to the sink.

   - Have guest paper towels in a tray on the counter if you're having multiple people over so they're not using your towel and not having to contend with a wet towel from repeated use.

8. Facilitate Connection
   - Introduce guests who don't know each other and offer light conversation starters or games if the group needs a little help mixing.

9. Keep It Real
   - Your home doesn't need to be perfect- authenticity and warmth go further than perfection. Guests will remember how they *felt*, not how spotless your floors were.

Tips for Hosting During the Day

It's a good idea to have a proper water pitcher and goblets so you can always offer your guest some water, but with an elevated twist. (Rummaging for a clean cup your family uses for everyday use needn't be so!)

Tips for Hosting Overnight

A small care basket in the bathroom or on their nightstand is a lovely touch. In terms of items for the basket, you can do whatever you want! Travel for work? You could use the basket as a repository of your unused collection of hotel soaps and lotions. Enjoy making things with your hands? You could make homemade bath salts, soaps, or candles. Short on time? Grab some lovely lotion, bath oils, essential oils, or candles the next time you're at the market. Add raffia to the bottom of the basket to help it look lush and full. An alternative to this could be tissue paper (you can spritz some lavender spray or perfume on it too!).

Options for Ambience

A beautiful-smelling home creates a welcoming, comforting atmosphere- and with so many options, it's easy to find what suits your space and style.

Candles are a classic go-to, offering warmth and ambiance. Pros: long-lasting scent, aesthetic appeal. Cons: open flame, can leave soot or be unsafe around kids or pets. If you like candles as much as I do, I highly recommend opting for jarred candles with a lid or investing in a candle snuffer. A wick trimmer is also a great tool to have on hand. Candles are so romantic and feel so old worldly, I think they're worth it.

Plug-ins like Glade are great for hands-off fragrance. Pros: continuous scent, low maintenance. Cons: artificial smell or intensity can be overwhelming to some, needs frequent replacement.

Room sprays offer an instant refresh. Pros: great for guests or a quick fix. Cons: short-lived and often need reapplying.

Diffusers (especially with essential oils) are a clean and stylish way to scent a room. Pros: no flame, customizable scents. Cons: not a very strong aroma, frequent refills and occasional cleaning.

Simmer pots (simmering citrus, herbs, and spices on the stove) fill your home with natural fragrance. Pros: cozy and non-toxic. Cons: short-term and need supervision

Fresh flowers like star gazer lilies not only look stunning but provide a natural, vibrant aroma. Pros: chemical-free and decorative. Cons: can trigger allergies, are perishable, and highly toxic to cats.

Whether you're aiming for subtle sophistication or bold fragrance, mixing and matching these options can help create the perfect scent story for your home.

"Do not forget to show hospitality to strangers, for by so doing some people have shown hospitality to angels without knowing it." Hebrews 13:2

Wreath Making

A friend once told me that every year at Christmas she tries to craft something with her own hands for her family. (Crafts? Crafts you say? You're speaking my language.) As a self-identified "indoor sports" kind of girl (no sports required or implied) this is something I have found so much joy and pleasure in as the years go by. I mainly find the time and the opportunity to be creative with crafting at Christmas time, but for me, no holiday or celebration is off limits. I love decorating with handmade wreaths. I've priced it out and I have found that for the quality and style of wreath I like to use in and around my home, it costs just as much for me to buy it as it does to make it. (Much to the dismay of my inner Fred Mertz.) Now, depending on the year or season and how much time I do or don't have, sometimes I'll buy them, but even then, I will typically add elements to the wreath as I love to make custom things for my home and family.

I could talk all day about crafting as there are so many different glorious forms, methods, and mediums, but for now, I wanted to share my love of wreath making. Wreaths are fabulous touches that adorn the doors and gates of your home, serve to welcome your guests, and give you a moment of joy as you come and go in your busy day.

The reality of wreaths is that while I wish they could last forever, and good materials will keep for several years, they do get weathered. The good news is, however, you can almost always reuse the wreath itself (most wreath structures are made of grape vines and these are very hearty). Then you can get to work creating your new wreath.

Because I may have a different wreath for a holiday vs. a season, I have found the need to store my wreaths well. I have four extra large size wreath bags that I hang from the rafters of my garage and have them organized by the seasons. I can store between 3-5 wreaths in each, and the bags keep them well preserved. The winter bag contains my Christmas wreaths, January wreath (white magnolias), and Valentine's wreath. My spring bag contains my spring wreath, Easter wreath, and a simple boxwood wreath I typically use around the time of St Patrick's Day. My summer bag contains a fourth of July vintage Americana wreath, a seashell wreath, and a lemon themed wreath. Finally, my fall wreath bag contains 2 fall themed wreaths, a grape themed wreath, and a cutesy Halloween wreath. (We do acknowledge Halloween in my family, but we hold it at an arm's length due to the holiday's origins, and we usually go to a carnival at our church anyway.)

Next, I'll share with you some ideas for making your own homemade wreath, no matter what season it is.

Spring Wreath

This spring wreath is beautiful and so simple to make. Here's how you can make it yourself.

Materials:
- 1 grapevine wreath in size of your choosing
- Floral wire
- Wire snips
- Hot glue gun
- Faux eggs
- Faux flowers, leaves, berries, and twigs, mini pinecones, or any other natural elements you want
- Wooden rosettes

Directions:
I always prop my wreaths up against something to create a 45° angle when I'm decorating. This gives me the most realistic vantage point that the wreath will have once hung on the door. Start decorating with your biggest element first, the eggs. Start at the top of your wreath and glue eggs to the wreath in a clockwise fashion, until you have as many as you prefer. Once your eggs are in place, begin working with your largest flowers, placing them around the wreath, and gluing where you want them. Then incorporate the rosettes and work your way down to the smallest elements you have and use them to fill in any gaps or spaces you don't like. Then stand back and marvel at what you just created!

Summer Wreath

This is an incredibly easy wreath to make, and this one is actually cheaper to make than purcahse, based on my experience. I like this style of wreath for summer particularly because it lasts longer than a floral wreath, which when exposed to the intense heat we have in the summer, can age after only a couple of seasons.

Materials:
- 1 fanned grapevine wreath in size of your choosing (you can either buy one that is white or spray paint one white)
- Floral wire
- Wire snips
- Hot glue gun
- Bag of assorted seashells from your local craft store, such as Michaels or Hobby Lobby

Directions:
Once your hot glue gun is ready to go, begin with your largest shells first and gue them to your wreath, going clockwise. Continue layering medium size shells, then small, then mini size seashells. You can add a small tie of ribbon if you'd like. Hang and enjoy!

Fall Wreath

I just love ushering in fall with home décor elements such as pumpkins, leaves, and cinnamon spice. This wreath is simple to make and will add charm to your home- season after season.

Materials:
- 1 fanned grapevine wreath in size of your choosing
- Faux floral stems (I really like using Windward silk flowers and I get mine at Aldik Home) but any type will do
- Leaf stems or greenery picks
- Other accents such as faux pumpkins, cinnamon sticks, etc.
- Fall themed ribbon
- Scissors

Directions:
Begin by placing your leaf stems and greenery first. Once you have them situated where you want them, glue them into place. Next add in your florals, designing with odd numbers and glue in place. Finally, add your accent pieces and once you have them where you want them, glue them into place. You can use fall themed ribbon to create a bow or to make a wreath hanger.

Winter Wreath

Crafting a winter wreath is a beautiful way to welcome the season and add warmth to your front door. With evergreens, pinecones, cinnamon, and a touch of sparkle or ribbon, it brings a festive, natural charm that celebrates the coziness of winter.

Materials:
- Evergreen wreath
- An assortment of pinecones
- Cinnamon sticks
- Gold ornaments or bells
- Floral wire
- Scissors

Directions:
Start with an evergreen wreath in a fabrication and size of your liking. Begin decorating by placing the natural elements around your wreath first (berries, fruits, etc.). Once you have arranged them to your liking, glue them down. Next you can layer in ornaments or other baubles of your choosing. Finally, you can finish it off with a gilded bow if you'd like.

Flower Arranging

When I was in my teens, I worked in the floral section of the local supermarket, and after that went on to work at a boutique florist in my hometown. Flowers do not have to be expensive to be good. If you have a good eye and invest a small amount of time up front to find out where the best flower sellers are in your community, you can save a ton of money on the back end as you use flowers to celebrate life's joyous moments. You can even use foraged pieces, or greenery clipped from your own yard to help bulk up arrangements. Most florists will charge per stem which can get pricey, but in my community we have a number of different markets and big box stores, so I've found some tricks to getting the most bang for my buck.

First of all, try to always buy a bouquet, and arrange it yourself at home in a vase before gifting. The mark up on floral arrangements once they've been paced into a vase is wild. Keep the vases from flowers that you've been given throughout the years and use those to give as gifts. With some Windex or Dawn dish soap they'll shine up like new and you'll be able to bring value and impact into your floral gift.

I've sleuthed around and found that I prefer to go to a local market for their bouquets of flowers, yet I am a die-hard fan of the roses at our local big box grocery store, Vons (Safeway in the Midwest). They import their roses from Ecuador, price them reasonably, and they last for weeks.

Flowers and their colors are known to symbolize sentiment and certain varieties to mark special occasions.

20 Common Flowers & Their Meanings

1. Carnation (pink) – A mother's love, gratitude, new birth (girl)
2. Chrysanthemum – Loyalty, longevity, friendship
3. Dahlia- Elegance, strength, creativity, and dignity
4. Daisy – Innocence, new beginnings, simplicity
5. Gardenia – Secret love, joy, refinement
6. Holly / Berries – goodwill, Christmas joy
7. Hydrangea – Gratitude, grace, heartfelt emotions, spring
8. Iris – Wisdom, hope, faith
9. Ivy – Fidelity, longevity, winter, Christmas, also spring
10. Lily (stargazer) – Ambition, encouragement, prosperity, friendship
11. Lily (trumpet) – Purity, rebirth, sympathy
12. Orchid – Beauty, strength, exotic elegance
13. Pansy – Thoughts
14. Peony – Prosperity, honor, romance
15. Pine- loyalty, longevity, Christmas joy
16. Rose (red) – Love, passion, romance, Christmas
17. Rose (white) – Purity, innocence, remembrance, sympathy
18. Sunflower – Adoration, loyalty, happiness, summer
19. Tulip – Perfect love, elegance, cheerfulness, spring, Easter
20. Zinnia – Lasting affection, endurance, remembrance of absent friends

Container Mediums, Floral Foams

Flower arranging is very creative, so don't feel constrained to use only vases to display your arrangements. You can use urns, baskets, buckets, pots, pitchers, vases, and bowls. Don't shy away from looking in cabinets and cupboards to find and use unique or unusual vessels, just choose a vessel that will best complement the flowers and the occasion. I like to use a number of different containers, but when I'm in a rush, my go-to is a crystal vase. For my wedding, I received my first real crystal vase ever from my husband's aunt and I was blown away by the stellar quality of a crystal (not a glass) vase. I don't pay retail prices for my vases. I keep an eye out for crystal vases at antique stores, thrift stores, or estate sales. I've been able to find some amazing Waterford crystal bud vases second-hand in my travels, for a fraction of their retail price.

There are some elements of floral design that are staples, and others that you can do without. Here are just a few:

Floral Tape

I usually just use good old scotch tape. My favorite type to work with both for making floral grids and giftwrapping is transparent, not the more common frosted.

Floral Foam

Floral foam comes in all shapes and sizes and can be used wet or dry (for faux flowers). I usually find myself buying it in squares or rectangles and cutting it to be the shape I want. Allow your foam to soak completely in a bath of water before using it with your real stems.

Other Materials

I recommend investing in a good pair of shears (but know that some rose varieties can be sensitive to bacteria and fungi that may be picked up on your blades, so having some rubbing alcohol on hand to wipe down your shears with can help prevent the spread of disease). Other materials to equip yourself with are; pipe cleaners, water picks, ribbon, cages, and wire.

Just a friendly note, it's important to know what you're working with when it comes to flowers, toxicity, pets, and young children.

Flower Arranging Rules

Always remember to cut your stems on a diagonal, so that there's a larger surface area for the flower to absorb water. This also makes it easier to insert the stem into floral foam, if you're working with it. When working with roses, use a knife to remove thorns and always remember that no floral leaves should be submerged underneath the waterline of your container, as they will breed bacteria and cause harm to the arrangement.

Don't be afraid to remove leaves from your flower stems. Keeping a few leaves here and there helps add a natural look to your arrangements, but all told, most leaves should go. To help woody stems (think hydrangea) absorb water optimally, crush each stem with a mallet and cut a slit several inches long with a knife.

In certain circumstances, you may find it necessary to work with a water pick. Water picks can be particularly useful when working with fussy flowers and arranging them in floral foam so you can ensure adequate water intake.

To preserve your handcrafted arrangements, add one or two drops of bleach to the water, and one teaspoon of sugar. When beginning a floral arranging project, prep your water first, then tape your vase. Once you're ready to begin, start with your greenery. From there, arrange the tallest stems first, and in the middle of your arrangement so that they provide a framework for the rest of your arrangement. Next, you'll wrap around the arrangement with medium blooms, and finish with the shorter and smaller blooms near the edges of the container. Interest comes from varying flower shapes and colors. Remember to design using stems in odd numbers, like 3 or 5 for example. You can always supplement garden flowers for purchased blooms to add variety and innovation. If you cut flowers from your garden, do so in the morning before the heat of the sun puts stress on them. I also advise positioning your finished arrangement away from direct sunlight to keep the flowers from wilting. If you're cutting flowers and stems from your garden, bring along a bucket or other container of water. Use sharp shears to cut the stem at an angle and immediately place them in water to prolong the life of the bloom.

Flowers should be harvested when they are newly opened, and the bud is just beginning to blossom. A tip I've come to learn is to actually cut the stems under water as you work to arrange their proper height in their vase (or another container). The reason for this is that doing so will allow water, not air, to be absorbed by the stem, therefore prolonging its life. In the next section,

I'll share some of my favorite seasonal arrangements with you along with instructions for how to make them.

Spring Silver

I love this arrangement. Trumpet lilies are known for their longevity so this arrangement should last almost two weeks. A note- stamen-bearing pollen inside the lilies will not only stain clothing but drop upon the petals, creating a messy look. To combat this, take a wet paper towel, draped over your fingertips, and using your fingers, reach into the flower, capturing each stamen, and pull up gently. The stamens will detach but won't cover you in pollen due to the moisture on the paper towel.

Materials:
- Trumpet lilies
- Eucalyptus (gunni variety)
- Baby's breath
- Queen Anne's lace
- Sterling silver footed bowl
- Floral foam

Directions:
1. Cut a block of dry floral foam to fit inside the bowl.
2. Soak the foam thoroughly in water and place back in the bowl.
3. Insert fully bloomed lilies in the foam, starting with the tallest stems first.
4. Fill in the open spaces with eucalyptus, Queen Anne's lace, baby's breath, and lilies with closed buds.

Delightful Summer Daisies

This is a unique and charming summer display for everyday use on your kitchen table. When I'm at the store and I don't have a specific occasion but have the hankering to buy some fresh flowers for the house, I get some daisies and whip up this carefree arrangement.

Materials:
- Daisies (white and yellow)
- Snapdragons
- Mums
- Glass vase

Directions:
1. Cut all stems under water and at a diagonal for optimal water absorption.
2. Create a grid at the mouth of your vase with some tape.
3. Prepare the water by adding a tablespoon of bleach.
4. Start with some tall stems of snapdragons and daisies first.
5. Then cut daisy and mum stems 2-3 inches shorter and arrange them around the interior of the mouth of the vase.
6. Next, add some mums closest to the mouth of the vase.
7. Fill in any holes you see with extra flowers.

Fall Flowers in a Pumpkin

To me, the colors of these flowers represent that final seasonal burst of heat as fall is ushered in. This arrangement looks great with smaller pumpkins or wheat placed around the base.

Materials:
- Sunflowers
- Goldenrods or chrysanthemums (orange)
- Mums
- Aster
- Gerbera daisy
- A pumpkin (variety of your choosing)
- Floral wire

Directions:
1. Cut the top off your pumpkin and hollow out the interior. Prepare the interior of the pumpkin with some bleach, and tape a grid at the opening.
2. Cut the mums and goldenrods (or chrysanthemums) to be the tallest stems (these should represent ¾ of the height of the pumpkin).
3. Then, arrange the sunflowers, mums, and aster.
4. Insert some floral wire through a few gerbera daisies and arrange them in any holes you may see.

Winter Berries in an Urn

Don't be intimidated by using a dome cage. These are easy to find online in the size you need to fit your urn, and you can wash and reuse it each time you make this arrangement. The dome shape adds to the elegance and is the secret ingredient to making a simple arrangement look very elaborate.

Materials:
- Ivy
- Roses (red and peach)
- Eucalyptus (seeded variety)
- Lisianthus
- Stems of raspberries on the vine (artificial)
- Hypericum (aka St. John's wort)
- Floral foam
- Dome cage (with spikes)
- Urn

Directions:
1. Cut a block of dry floral foam to fit inside the urn.
2. Soak the foam thoroughly in water and place back into the urn. Set the dome cage on top.
3. Insert the greenery first, followed by the roses, artificial raspberries, lisianthus, and St. John's Wort.
4. Fill in any empty spaces with more greenery and St. John's wort.

Chapter 6
Tablescapes

"In my Father's house are many mansions: if it were not so, I would have told you. I go to prepare a place for you. And if I go and prepare a place for you, I will come again, and receive you unto myself; that where I am, there you may be also." John 14:1-3

Preparing a Place

Ah, my absolute favorite aspect of homemaking- tablescapes! My dining table is a sacred place to me and has a different tableau for each holiday, season, and special occasion (such as birthdays and other celebrations). I think there is something so gracious and lovely about having your dining table set to celebrate the season or holiday. Tablescapes help me establish traditions in the home and build memories for my family as we enjoy a prepared table. I know that for busy families with working parents and school aged children, the dining table can become the catch-all, communal space for the day-to-day maelstrom, but it doesn't have to be. At my house, homework is done on clipboards or at small desks in bedrooms. I figure my children's "job" is to go to school as mine is to work, so why not equip them with everything they need, in their own space? And mail? Well, that's my job, so it goes on my desk. Packages? Opened and broken down and taken within a day to the trashcans by my loving husband who takes his responsibility of taking out the trash so seriously, he put it in his wedding vows. (What can I say, I'm a lucky lady.) Come dinnertime, we use the plates that are on the table, my oldest washes them, and before I go to bed, I place them back on the table so it can be complete in its gracious greeting of us once we wake up in the morning.

Hospitality doesn't require extravagance- only intention. As Christian hosts, we can see each meal as an act of stewardship, a way to embody God's hospitality in tangible ways. The linens we lay, the candles we light, the dishes we choose- they're all expressions of care and love. When we serve from a place of peace and purpose, the table becomes a special space.

The topic of tablescapes is such a visual and intuitive subject it may seem overwhelming, but when broken down, it offers the rich opportunity for storytelling, beauty, and inspiration. In a world that rushes past meals and multitasks through moments, the act of preparing a place- with care, grace, and intention- can become a quiet kind of ministry. It's a way of saying, *I see you. You're welcome here. You belong.* Just as our Heavenly Father prepares a table before us (Psalm 23:5), we too are invited to prepare spaces that nourish not only the body, but also the heart. A tablescape is about blessing. It's about transforming the everyday into the extraordinary through love and a touch of beauty. My hope through the pages of this chapter is that your tables would become places that reflect not just your taste, but your testimony. And that every seat would remind someone: *there is room for you here. Welcome Home.* May your table be a place of laughter, connection, and elegance.

The Table as a Canvas of Grace

You don't need a big budget to create something beautiful and meaningful. We'll explore how to design meaningful, beautiful tablescapes that honor both occasion and spirit- no perfection required. Start with what you already have and build from there. For example, a pitcher with gerbera daisies and a checkered tablecloth is a classic, great place to start. You can always be thoughtful and add personal touches to your vignette. Remember beauty is in the intention, not the price tag.

Whether it's a simple weekday dinner or a grand holiday feast, the way we adorn our table reflects the heart we have for those seated around it. Some such personal touches you can incorporate include;

• Place cards with scripture (I have chosen refurbished wine corks as my place card holders for year-round use). I've found that no matter how formal my table may be, this theme carries over nicely no matter what the occasion is. Additionally, I always use place cards anytime I'm hosting anyone outside of my immediate family. Doing so takes the guesswork out of your guests' experience and makes mealtime flow more seamlessly. It also shows your consideration for them and their dining experience.

• Handwritten menu cards (Hester & Cook make some beautiful ones that coordinate with their designer paper placemats. I use these anytime I'm hosting a large gathering, so guests know what they're having.)

• Conversation starter "prompts" interwoven into the tablescape. I like to do these at every holiday gathering to get people talking about seasonally specific topics. These can be a nice fall back if there's a lull in the conversation.

• Seasonal elements incorporated into the setting. This could look like a sprig of lavender, evergreen, or a tulip tucked in to each napkin ring. I'm also a big fan of seasonal menus so feel free to incorporate what you're cooking with too! Think of pumpkins and gourds or (edible) flowers. See Chapter 8 for my Edible Flower Guide.

• When putting together your tablescape concepts, think in layers- a runner, chargers, plates, napkins, flatware, a centerpiece. Layering adds depth and interest. Below are some foundational elements of table setting.

The Essentials

- Table linens- a white or cream tablecloth or runner, even a piece of fabric, can anchor your setting and soften the space. If you have a showstopper of a table or don't want to cover it, opt to use linen napkins to add softness to the tableau. (To preserve my linen napkins, and to add depth and warmth, I always add a rectangular, themed paper napkin to my napkin ring holders on top of my cloth napkins.) I also have both gold and silver monogrammed paper napkins I buy in bulk which are great to use when I'm short on time and they also double as guest bathroom napkins. Because I don't have unlimited real estate or resources, I have chosen crystal napkin ring holders as my signature look. They go with every occasion and look gorgeous.

- Centerpieces – floral arrangements (faux or real), greenery, fruit bowls, candles — anything that draws the eye and evokes the season or occasion. Just remember to be aware of the height of your centerpiece, that it won't get in the way of people talking.

- Place settings – plates, utensils, and glasses don't always have to match. You can mix and match heirlooms, thrifted finds, or everyday dishes. I have found that the easiest print to do this with and still maintain versatility is floral patterns. For my family's everyday dishes, I have adopted a French countryside style of plate. They're off-white and just subdued enough to be proper for daily use, but they can get gussied up for a themed table in no time. And to help me bring my themes to life, I rely on Hester and Cook's high-end paper placemats.

I know that recently "hosting closets" have become popular, and I am a huge fan of the idea. I don't live in a home that has that much closet space though, so I have carved out little sections of space to store my pieces. This is why I share that by sticking to whites and creams for plates and dishes, your tablescape centerpieces and accents are the only things you need to find storage for. Additionally, the paper place mats I use take up a fraction of the space fabric ones do. I've also selected one sterling silver, and one crystal salt and pepper set which go with any themed tablescape I'm putting together.

I must confess, my caveat to the neutral tone dishes to hack storage space constraints is Christmas and Easter. I decided that it was worth it to me to contend with the storage situation at my home to have a Spode brand classic Christmas tree set for Christmas, and Bordallo Pinheiro cabbage plates for Easter.

Other personal touches – handwritten place cards, a praise and gratitude card during holidays or a sprig of rosemary tied with twine show your guests they were thought of. I've recently incorporated crystal knife rests into my tablescape and I highly recommend them. Also, I will mold pats of butter in thick silicone Cameo molds and slightly freeze to set so that each guest has their own personal butter pat, and a place to set their knife. I have found this makes a meal move more smoothly so people aren't leaving their knives behind with the butter or taking the communal knife by mistake.

Types of Tablescapes

- Everyday elegance
- Seasonal or holiday
- Themed celebrations (birthday, harvest dinner, baby shower, etc.)

A Word on Seasonal Inspiration…

Let God's creation be your guide. Each season offers fresh colors, textures, and meaning. The following are some examples of how you can incorporate the beauty of each season on your table:

Spring: florals, garden greens, blushes and creams. Think: renewal, light, and life.

Summer: al fresco dining, bold colors, citrus tones, woven textures, coastal elements.

Welcome Home: *A Guide to Homemaking, From the Heart*

Fall: rustic textures, foliage, candles, pumpkins, and harvest tones.
A season for gratitude and gathering.

Winter: cozy textiles, evergreens, warm metals like white and gold, cozy textures.
Think: warmth, quiet, light in darkness.

Creating Beauty with What You Have

You don't need to purchase anything new to set a beautiful table. Some of the loveliest designs come from improvisation and creativity, and a well-stocked cache:

- Nature: clip branches, herbs, or blooms from your yard.
- Kitchen: use lemons, apples, or bread as part of the centerpiece.
- Candles: always a classic. I recommend buying them in bulk and keeping white, cream, and red on hand. Candlestick holders in a few fabrications are a staple too: silver, gold, glass (more casual) and crystal (for elegant events).

Centering Christ at the Table

Your table can also reflect your faith in subtle or symbolic ways:

- Place a candle in the center to represent Christ's presence in your home.
- Include a verse or blessing at each place setting. (My favorite blessing is Numbers 6:24-26 "The Lord bless you, and keep you, the Lord make his face shine upon you, and be gracious to you, the Lord turn his face toward you and give you peace." I actually have this inscribed on a sterling silver bracelet ever present on my right wrist.)
- Begin the meal with a prayer to ask God's blessing over the meal.
- These practices need not be elaborate or formal- they simply remind us that He is the true Host. These little rituals, repeated over time, become the fabric of family tradition.

When Things Aren't Picture Perfect

Real life is messy. The roast burns. The centerpiece wilts. The kids spill juice. And yet, grace abounds. Like I said, hospitality isn't about perfection. It's about presence. Something I have to tell the recovering perfectionist in me is to host with grace, not perfection. When your heart is open, your home becomes a haven- no matter what the table looks like. Let the table be a reflection of the freedom you've found in Christ, not a pursuit of picture-perfect hosting. Beauty matters, but love matters most.

Your Tablescape Toolkit

Here's a list of 10 must-have versatile items to have in stock:

1. A white tablecloth or neutral runner
2. Glass or ceramic candle holders
3. A set of cloth napkins in natural tones (white, cream), and themed paper napkins
4. Simple white plates
5. Wood or woven chargers
6. Gold and silver chargers
7. Votive candles or tapers
8. A few crystal or ceramic vases for centerpieces
9. Faux flowers that tie in to the color story of your dining area
10. Crystal or glass goblets

These pieces mix effortlessly with seasonal accents or personal touches.
Keep these items on hand, and you'll always be ready to set a beautiful, meaningful table.

Reminders

• Budget-friendly beauty is possible! Start where you are, build a stunning table with what you have. You can always go high-low and splurge on some items, then go cheap on others.

• Layer textures and ensure you incorporate a good mix of linens, wood, ceramics, glass, and greenery.

• Mix old and new: heirloom pieces with modern finds. Special finds at a vintage shop or antique store make for great conversation pieces.

• Don't forget the power of candles and lighting. Set ambiance with soft piano or classical music or praise and worship as you dine.

• Use nature in your décor. Incorporate foraged branches, herbs, flowers, and fruit. Don't be afraid to cut off a branch and style it in a vase or pot to accentuate seasonality in your home.

An Invitation to Make Room

In closing, every time we set the table, we make room- for connection, for comfort, for the Spirit to move. Whether it's a holiday feast or a weekend breakfast, each gathering becomes a special opportunity to show love. Jesus didn't merely perform miracles at feasts; He *was* the feast. The Host and the nourishment. May our tables reflect this truth: that in our homes, as in our hearts, there is always room for one more.

Chapter 7
In the Kitchen

"Blessed are those who hunger and thirst for righteousness, for they will be satisfied."
Matthew 5:6

I don't like anybody in my kitchen. I know, I know. At least I take comfort in knowing I'm not the only one. My stepdad shares stories of his childhood and his mother hollering at his father "Herb, get your size 13 triple-E shoes out of my kitchen" while she was preparing dinner. In my defense, I think it's a creative thing. When I'm in the kitchen I'm thinking, I'm working with my hands, I'm reading recipes, I'm making a mess (and cleaning it up as I go along, which is very important when cooking), so I really don't want to have to maneuver around others. I take pride and joy in feeding my family. It is one of the most inherently feminine things we do. Think about it, our bodies were created by God to literally feed another human being. I find much joy in feeding my family, and telling them to get out of the kitchen.

A word on preservation and food waste…food waste drives me nuts. If there's a way I can avoid it, I will. I was raised by "clean your plate" kind of parents and while I don't do that with my children because I don't want to encourage overeating, I do store and save food regularly. It also helps us save money on our grocery bill. I had an aunt tell me once, "In life, it's not about how much you make, it's how much you *save*."

I think every household should have a sturdy, matching set of Tupperware. (Best if it's glass, but BPA-free plastic will suffice.) I also recommend investing in square Tupperware, as circular Tupperware takes up more storage space, both on the shelf and in the fridge.

To keep your produce fresh longest, don't wash with water before putting into your crisper. Water encourages bacteria growth and will age your produce.

Take your bananas apart when you put them in your fruit bowl, if you leave them connected at the stem they'll ripen faster. And this way, they're even easier for hungry kiddos to grab as a healthy snack.

Place fruits in one crisper drawer of your fridge and your vegetables in the other. Many fruits (including tomatoes) give off ethylene gas which speeds up a vegetable's decay. Now if you're hoping to speed up the ripening of fruits, place them in a paper bag along with an apple. The apple will give off ethylene gas and speed up the process nicely.

Store your opened chunks of cheese in aluminum foil, they will stay fresh much longer and not mold. I always store my bread in the fridge, it keeps it fresh so much longer. Bread also freezes beautifully. To reheat refrigerated bread (biscuits, rolls, scones, or muffins), place them in the microwave with a cup of water. The increased moisture will keep the bread moist and help it reheat faster.
If you have berries that are unripe or bland, sprinkle a pinch of salt and sugar onto freshly cut berries before serving to enhance their flavor and bring out their juiciness. Are your berries starting to look listless? Soak them in a bowl filled with ice water for 10-20 minutes and they will perk back up.

Helpful Tips for Freezer Storage

Many people don't know that you can freeze a myriad of foods to preserve them, without sacrificing their texture or flavor; dairy, butter, milk, coffee creamer, and cheese are things I regularly freeze at my house. Fish and seafood can be frozen raw, or prepared, and will spring back to life beautifully.

Sometimes you just can't get through all the fruit you have on hand. Berries (washed and hulled) freeze great and can come back to serve you in a smoothie or protein shake. Stone fruits such as peaches, nectarines, and plums are great frozen, and even apple slices too. I freeze my apples once they've been washed, skinned, and sliced and use them in apple pies or smoothies and juices. I would steer clear of freezing citrus fruits though. Their structure and texture don't hold up.

Hearty vegetables such as carrots, radishes, and other root vegetables freeze well, as well as cruciferous veggies like broccoli and cauliflower. If you plan to sauté veggies then freeze them, things like snap peas, eggplant, bell peppers, and mushrooms freeze well. In my experience, celery does not freeze well. Due to its high water content, it freezes all the way through and retains no structure once thawed. I freeze whole loaves of bread, bags of rolls, hotdog and hamburger buns all the time so they don't go bad.

To help lessen food waste in your kitchen and to help you prepare for each week so meals don't take more of your time than they need to, I've created a Weekly Menu Planner, complete with a grocery shopping list section that you can download for free on my website: www.welcomehomebygina.com.

A note about air fryers… recently someone asked me what I use an air fryer for, and this was coming from a self-proclaimed foodie! I muffled my gasp and said, everything. In their mind, they thought it was only best for the things for which it's most marketed for: like chicken wings and French fries. It's true it is great for those things, but it is also fabulous for everything else. And with some models, you can even bake a cake in them (although I have not done this, my preferred cake baking method is the oven, no matter how hot it may make my kitchen in the summer). So, I thought I'd include a note on the magic that is the air fryer. I cook chicken breast, steak, shrimp, crisp up leftover pizza, chicken nuggets, pizza bites, pizza rolls (the kids love pizza), vegetables, potatoes, sweet potatoes, zucchini, roasted tomatoes on the vine, eggplant parmesan, skewers, the list goes on.

And the beauty is that, unlike cooking on your stove top which requires your time and attention, and to be perfectly honest, so many weeknights I just don't have either, you can set it and go do something else, like take a shower and wash your hair while you cook dinner for your family. It also won't heat your kitchen or home, which makes it your best, most fabulous friend in the summer months.

Substitutions for Common Ingredients

If you're anything like me, you may find yourself asking your family to stay in line at the market while you run back for one last item you need (a personal pet peeve of my husband's) only to get home and realize you still forgot something. I admit I am still training my family to add things we are out of to the grocery list on the fridge. As a busy mama, I typically have only one shot at a project (cooking, baking, flower arranging, planting, gift wrapping) as there's just no time for rework. So, I created a handy little list of perfectly suitable substitutions when you realize you're out of something.

Item	Amount	Substitution
Allspice	1 teaspoon	½ tsp cinnamon & 1/8 tsp ground cloves
Baking powder	1 teaspoon	¼ tsp baking soda & 5/8 tsp cream of tartar
Buttermilk	1 cup	1 cup plain yogurt
Cream, heavy	1 cup	¾ cup milk 7 1/3 cup melted butter (this won't whip up)
Cream, whipping	1 cup	2/3 cup well-chilled evaporated milk, whipped
Honey	1 cup	1 ¼ cups sugar & ½ cup liquid (of whatever is called for in the recipe, i.e. oil, water)
Lemon juice	1 teaspoon	½ tsp vinegar
Milk, whole	1 cup	½ cup evaporated milk & ½ cup of water or 1 cup skim milk & 2 tsp melted butter
Sugar, granulated	1 cup	1 cup firmly packed brown sugar
Tomatoes, canned	1 cup	½ cup tomato sauce, ½ cup water, or 1 1/3 cups chopped fresh tomatoes, simmered
Tomato juice	1 cup	½ cup tomato sauce, ½ cup water, & a dash each of salt and sugar
Tomato ketchup	½ cup	½ cup tomato sauce, 2 Tbsp sugar, 1 Tbsp vinegar, & 1/8 tsp ground cloves

Appetizers

Something I think is important to address is the timing for appetizers when hosting a meal or a gathering. I fully realize that different cultures relate to time (and specifically social time) differently, and at the same time, my rule of thumb is to have drinks and appetizers ready at the start time of your event(s).

A note here on invitations if I may, whether invitations are sent via email, text, or traditional card by mail (my favorite!) it's always a good idea to put the start and end time of the event. I've found that people in general enjoy certainty and tend to appreciate knowing when it's ok to arrive, and at what time the hostess has planned for the event to conclude, because then she's got dishes to wash!

By the same token, I recommend place cards at table settings. This quick extra step before your event has begun ensures you're able to put together the most suitable seating arrangements, and guests appreciate having the guesswork taken out of where to sit and who they'll be sitting with. Not to mention, it's such a sophisticated way to set a table.

Peruvian Ceviche

This recipe belonged to my father-in-law, Miguel, who grew up in the small beach town of Callao, just outside Lima on Peru's west coast. Taught to cook by his mother, he carried on her tradition with heart and skill. He is now in the presence of our Lord. Prep time: 20 minutes. Cooking time: 15 minutes.

Ingredients:
- Peruvian aji yellow chili paste
- Shrimp, uncooked
- White fish (tilapia or red snapper), uncooked
- 1 bag of limes
- 2-3 big lemons
- 1/2 purple onion, chopped
- 1/2 bunch of fresh cilantro, chopped
- 1 package imitation crab meat
- 1 serrano pepper, minced
- 2 avocados, cubed
- Salt and pepper, to taste
- Flat tostada shells

Directions:
1. Juice all the limes and lemons into a bowl. Add the uncooked fish and shrimp. The fish and shrimp will cure / cook in only 10-15 minutes in the citrus juice.
2. Add the chopped cilantro, serrano pepper, onion, 1 Tbsp of chili paste (to taste) and salt and pepper.
3. Use the avocado as garnish.
4. Place on top of tostada shells and enjoy!

Bean Dip Olé

Creamy, hearty, and packed with flavor, this bean dip is the perfect way to kick off any gathering. Whether you're hosting a casual game night or a festive holiday spread, this crowd-pleaser pairs beautifully with chips, veggies, or warm tortillas—and it comes together in minutes! (Yields about 2 cups.)

Ingredients:
- 13oz package cream cheese
- 1 cup refried beans
- ½ cup sour cream
- 2 Tbsp minced green pepper
- 2 Tbsp minced white onion
- 2 oz diced green chilies
- 2 tsp chili sauce
- 1 tsp chili powder
- ½ tsp Worcestershire sauce
- 1 Tbsp taco sauce
- Salt and pepper, to taste
- Hot sauce (your choice), to taste

Directions:
1. In a medium bowl, mash the cream cheese well with a fork. Then blend in refried beans.
2. Add the remaining ingredients and blend thoroughly.
3. Refrigerate for at least three hours.

Serve with tortilla chips or chopped vegetables.

Ranch Spinach Dip

This classic spinach dip is rich, creamy, and irresistibly satisfying- perfect for spreading, scooping, or sharing. Whether served warm or chilled, it's a timeless appetizer that brings comfort and flavor to any table.

Ingredients:
- 1 package of Hidden Valley Original Ranch salad dressing mix
- 2 cups (1 pint) sour cream
- 1 package (10 oz) frozen, chopped spinach, cooked and drained
- ¼ cup onion, minced
- ¾ tsp basil
- ½ tsp oregano
- Salt and pepper, to taste

Directions:
1. Combine ingredients. Start to blend. Chill for at least 1 hour.
2. Serve in hollowed out round loaf of French or sourdough bread.
3. Use hollowed out section to make bread cubes for dipping.

Salads & Dressings

Summer Salad with Watermelon, Feta and Cucumber

Light, refreshing, and bursting with flavor, this summer salad pairs juicy watermelon with refreshing cucumber and feta for the perfect balance of sweet and savory. It's a colorful, cooling appetizer that celebrates the best of the season in every bite. (Total prep time: 10 minutes. Serves 4.)

Ingredients:
- 3 cups of watermelon, cubed or balls
- 1 ½ cup sliced Persian cucumbers
- 2 Tbsp fresh mint leaves, thinly sliced
- 1/3 cup feta cheese
- 3 Tbsp olive oil
- 1 Tbsp lime juice
- Salt and pepper, to taste

Directions:
1. Place the prepared watermelon, cucumber and mint in a large bowl.
2. In a small bowl, whisk together the olive oil, lime juice, and salt and pepper.
3. Drizzle the dressing over the melon mixture and toss to coat.
4. Sprinkle with feta cheese and serve!

Avocado Veggie Salad

My sister-in-law Jess gave me this recipe. This salad is so fresh and delicious, and it's a breeze to put together for a potluck or a picnic, or to serve alongside dinner. The recipe is designed to be made in equal parts, so if you're feeding a crowd, just double it.

Ingredients:
- 2 avocados, cubed
- 2 English cucumbers, cubed
- 2 pints of cherry tomatoes, cut in half
- 1 red onion
- 1 lemon (optional)
- Salt and pepper, to taste

Directions:
1. Combine equal parts of cubed avocados, cubed English cucumber, cherry tomatoes, cut in half, and chopped white onion.
2. Then add creamy balsamic dressing (Briana's brand is our family's favorite).
3. Garnish with salt and pepper.
4. To brighten this bowl of glorious goodness even more, you can squeeze lemon juice on top.
5. Mix and serve up!

Homemade Buttermilk Ranch Dressing

Cool, creamy, and full of herby goodness, this homemade ranch dressing is a versatile staple perfect for dipping, drizzling, or dressing up any dish. Once you've made it from scratch, you'll never go back to the bottled kind!

Ingredients:
- ½ cup mayonnaise
- ¼ cup sour cream
- 2 tsp dried chives
- 1/2 tsp dried parsley
- 1/2 tsp garlic powder
- 1/8 tsp black pepper, ground
- 1/2 tsp fresh dill
- 1/2 tsp onion powder
- 1/3 cup milk
- 1/3 cup heavy cream of choice (half-and-half is ok)

Directions:
1. Whisk together in a mixing bowl. Enjoy!

Great Grandma E's Herb Dressing

Bright, zesty, and bursting with garden-fresh flavor, this herb dressing brings a vibrant touch to salads, veggies, and grilled appetizers. It's a simple way to elevate any dish with the taste of fresh-picked herbs.

Ingredients:

- 1/2 cup vinegar
- 1 – 1 ½ cups of extra-virgin olive oil
- 1 ½- 2 cups of granulated sugar
- 2 1/2 tsp salt
- 1 tsp mustard
- Dash of paprika
- Dash of dried bay leaf
- Dashes of all; Lawry's seasoned salt, onion salt, garlic salt, and celery salt

Directions:

1. Mix all ingredients together well.

Note: The sugar will not all dissolve and will make this dressing thick so mix well and pour over salad just before serving. This quantity keeps well in the fridge a long time.

Nana's Honey Mustard Dressing

With the perfect balance of sweetness and spice, this honey mustard dressing is a bold and versatile favorite. Ideal for dipping, drizzling, or marinating, it adds a flavorful punch to everything from crisp veggies to tender chicken.

Ingredients:
- 1 1/2 cup mayonnaise
- 1/4 cup honey
- 1/4 cup mustard
- 1/4 cup extra virgin olive oil
- 1 Tbsp white vinegar
- 1/2 tsp onion powder
- 1/4 tsp red pepper flakes

Directions:
1. Mix all ingredients together.

Makes 2 1/4 cups of dressing.

Chinese Chicken Salad

Crisp, colorful, and full of crunch, this Chinese Chicken Salad is a refreshing blend of tender chicken, shredded cabbage, and a zesty sesame-ginger dressing. It's a perfect harmony of textures and flavors that's light enough for lunch yet satisfying enough for dinner.

Ingredients:

- 1 pound of cooked chicken
- 1 head of iceberg lettuce
- 4 stocks of green onions, chopped
- ½ bag of shredded carrots
- 2 Tbsp of toasted almonds, chopped
- 2 Tbsp of sesame seeds, toasted
- 10 oz can of mandarin oranges
- Wontons, to taste

Dressing:

- 2 Tbsp sugar
- 1 tsp salt
- 1/2 tsp of fresh cracked pepper
- 1/4 cup avocado oil
- 3 Tbsp of vinegar
- 1 Tbsp of sesame oil

Mix well in a bowl.

Directions:

1. Add salad ingredients to a bowl, toss with dressing and serve. Enjoy!

Mains

Having been born and raised in Southern California, I have had the privilege and opportunity to explore many types of cuisines. I love to learn about other cultures and see how other people live, and I think cooking is one of the ways to do that. I have assembled a collection of favorite recipes that include Peruvian, Mexican, French, Asian, Persian, Indian, American and Italian dishes. It is a pride and joy to me. I am so happy to be able to share some of the very best with you. Each of these recipes carries with it a memory- of a loved one's kitchen, a special celebration, or a new flavor discovered on an ordinary day. Some were passed down through generations, while others were gathered during meaningful conversations or travels. What unites them all is the heart behind them. These dishes have nourished not just bodies, but relationships, and it brings me so much joy to invite you into that experience. May these recipes inspire you to try something new, gather around the table with those you love, and celebrate the beauty of connection through food.

Gina Romero

Poultry

Chicken Dasgupta

Fragrant, flavorful, and richly spiced, this Indian chicken dish brings the warmth and depth of traditional spices to your table. Whether served with rice or naan, it's a comforting entrée that celebrates the bold, aromatic essence of Indian cuisine.

Ingredients:

- 2 Tbsp butter
- 1 Tbsp curry powder
- 1 apple (granny smith)
- 1 yellow onion
- 1 can cream of mushroom soup (such as Campbell's)
- 1 cup heavy cream (or substitute 1 can evaporated skim milk)
- About 3 pounds of chicken thighs (marinated ahead of time with garlic, soy sauce, paprika, and salt)
- Basmati rice
- Green beans

Directions:

1. Preheat oven to 350°F. Sauté the curry powder in the butter.
2. Finely chop the apple and onion, then add to the butter and curry. Cook until the onion is transparent on medium heat.
3. Add mushroom soup and cream (or evaporated skim milk) to the curry mixture.
4. Arrange chicken in a single layer in a greased 9"x13" baking dish, sprinkle with paprika, and pour the sauce over the chicken.
5. Bake uncovered, at 350°F for about 90 minutes.
6. Prepare the rice.
7. Sautee the green beans with butter, garlic, and salt.

Serve the chicken over rice with green beans on the side.

Las Posadas Enchiladas

Ingredients:

- 1 ½ cups cooked, shredded chicken (I recommend getting a grocery store rotisserie chicken to shred. It's cheap, saves time, and the chicken is predictably juicy.)
- 1 can (19oz) La Victoria brand red enchilada sauce, divided (this is my favorite brand)
- 1 can (4.5oz) chopped green chiles
- 1 white onion, chopped (a tip- if you put the onion in the fridge and chop it cold, it won't sting your eyes)
- 1 tomato, diced (for garnish)
- 3 green onions, chopped (for garnish)
- 1 cup (4 oz) shredded Monterey jack cheese
- ½ cup slivered almonds
- 1/8 tsp cinnamon
- ¼ cup olive oil (or substitute avocado oil)
- 1 package of 6-inch corn tortillas (you won't use the whole package)
- Sour cream
- Hot sauce of your choosing (can substitute with taco sauce)

Directions:

1. Heat oven to 350°F. In a medium bowl, combine shredded chicken, 1/3 cup enchilada sauce, green chiles, cheese, onions, almonds, and cinnamon.
2. In a frying pan, heat olive oil at medium heat and dip each tortilla in the oil, slightly crisping on each side (in my frying pan I do 3 at a time). Then dip each tortilla in reserved enchilada sauce.
3. In a baking dish, begin to assemble the enchiladas, spooning ¼ cup chicken mixture down the center, roll up. Place seam side down in a baking dish. Layer until dish is almost full.
4. Pour the remaining enchilada sauce over the top. Bake at 350°F for 25 mins. Garnish with sour cream, tomatoes, and green onions.

Chicken Cordon Bleu

Ingredients:
- 4 skinless, boneless chicken breast halves
- 6 slices of Swiss cheese
- 4 slices of cooked ham
- Shredded mozzarella cheese for topping the chicken
- ½ cup seasoned bread crumbs
- ¼ tsp salt
- 1/8 tsp ground black pepper
- Parchment paper
- Toothpicks

Directions:
1. Preheat oven to 350°F. Pound chicken breasts into ¼ inch thickness with a mallet.
2. Rub each side of the chicken with salt and pepper. Place 1 piece of cheese and 1 slice of ham on top of each breast.
3. Roll up each breast and secure in pace with a toothpick. Sprinkle chicken evenly with breadcrumbs.
4. Wrap in parchment paper (this keeps the moisture in while baking).
5. Bake for 30-35 minutes or until chicken is no longer pink. (Chicken is considered cooked when it registers at 165°F on a meat thermometer.)
6. Remove from oven and place mozzarella cheese on top of each breast. Return to oven for 3-5 minutes or until cheese has melted. Remove toothpicks and serve immediately.

I serve this dish with mashed potatoes and a green salad.

Persian-Style Pomegranate Chicken

This recipe is loosely based on the traditional Persian dish Faisinjan and is so flavorful. (Total time 1 hour and 30 minutes.)

Ingredients:
- 1 whole chicken, cut into 8 pieces
- 6 pomegranates
- 1 cup toasted pine nuts or walnuts (finely chopped)
- 1 Tbsp lemon juice
- 2 Tbsp honey
- 1 tsp cinnamon
- ½ tsp cumin
- 1 yellow onion, sliced thinly
- 3 Tbsp olive oil
- 1 cup plain yogurt
- 1 grapefruit (for 1/2 cup grapefruit juice)
- 1 Tbsp powdered sugar
- 4 cups of cooked saffron rice pilaf (Parsi Pulao)

Directions:
1. Juice 5 of the pomegranates by cutting them in half and scoop out the seeds and press them through a sieve. (To avoid juice splatters, you can peel them open submerged in a bowl of water). Remove the seeds from one pomegranate to use as garnish. Heat the olive oil in a large skillet over high heat.
2. Salt and pepper the chicken and place into skillet. Cook the chicken just enough to lightly brown on all sides. Remove the chicken to a platter and set aside. Pour off all the oil from the skillet except for 1 tablespoon. Turn the heat to medium and add the onions. Cook the onions until soft, about 3-4 minutes.
3. Add the nuts and cook an additional minute. Whisk in the pomegranate juice, lemon juice, honey, cinnamon, and cumin. Add the chicken back to the pan. Bring the mixture to a simmer and continue to cook until chicken is done, about 45 minutes to an hour.
4. Cook the rice pilaf. In a small bowl, whisk together the yogurt, powdered sugar, and grapefruit juice. It should have the consistency of mayonnaise.
5. Serve up the rice pilaf on each plate, add the chicken on top, and pour some of the pomegranate sauce over the chicken and rice. Add a dollop of yogurt on top and sprinkle a few pomegranate seeds around the plate for garnish.

Beef

Stuffed Bell Peppers

I love bell peppers. They are so versatile and taste great. Bell peppers with 3 bumps on the bottom are sweeter, and better for eating, whereas peppers with 4 bumps on the bottom are firmer and better for cooking.

Ingredients:

- 4 bell peppers (choose an array of green, red, yellow, orange)
- 1 pound ground hamburger meat (can substitute for turkey)
- 1 yellow onion, chopped
- 1 can black beans
- 1 can of corn
- 1 cup cooked rice
- ½ can tomato sauce
- 2 smashed garlic cloves
- Kosher salt and black pepper
- Paprika
- Olive oil
- Shredded cheese (your choice)
- Fresh parsley for garnish (optional)

Directions:

1. Cut the tops off the bell peppers and save. De-vein and remove all seeds. Set aside in a baking pan for later use. Turn oven on to 375°F. Put some olive oil in a heated pan on the stove top. Place onions in the pan, season with kosher salt. Let the onions cook till tender before adding the other vegetables, then cook 3-4 minutes.
2. Add more olive oil to the vegetables and season with more salt and pepper. Remove the cooked vegetables from the skillet and put in the ground meat. Season with plenty of salt and pepper and some paprika. Brown the meat in the pan, then add the vegetables back in and add the tomato sauce.
3. Cook the rice next. Add the garlic, turn the heat off, and give the mixture an extra stir to check the liquid content. If it's not to your liking, add more tomato sauce.
4. Stuff the mixture into the bell peppers. Top with shredded cheese. Put the tops of the bell peppers on. Add any leftover tomato sauce to the baking dish so the peppers don't stick the bottom. Cook at 375°F for approximately 20 minutes. Enjoy!

Lomo Saltado

This awesome dish hails from Peru and is as simple as it is delicious. It was my father-in-law's authentic recipe. You can throw it together within minutes, and you don't need much.

Ingredients:

- 18 ounces sirloin steak, cut into strips or cubes
- 1 red onion, chopped into chunky slices
- 2 tomatoes, chopped into eight slices
- 1 aji amarillo chili pepper, sliced finely, veins and seeds removed (or 1 yellow pepper- Serrano)
- 1 tsp fresh garlic
- 2 Tbsp olive oil
- 20 ounces white rice, cooked
- 11 oz thick potato slices ready for frying (Yukon gold or use frozen steak cut French fries)
- 1/2 cup beef stock
- 4 Tbsp soy sauce
- 4 Tbsp white vinegar
- A handful of cilantro leaves
- 1/4 tsp oregano, ground
- 1 tsp black pepper, freshly crushed
- 1 tsp cumin
- Ground salt, to taste

Directions

1. Heat the pan. Fry the potato slices in the vegetable oil and set aside until needed.
2. Cut the sirloin steak into strips, marinate them in the cumin, salt, the 4 Tbsp of vinegar, 1 Tbsp of olive oil, black pepper, and the soy sauce for 10 minutes before cooking.
3. Bring a Tbsp of olive oil to a very high heat in a frying pan. Strain and remove the steak strips from the marinade and fry them over a high heat for around 4-5 minutes or until sealed
4. Add the onion, chili pepper and garlic to the pan. Fry for 1 minute while continuously moving the frying pan and add the beef stock.
5. Add the tomato and fry the ingredients in the pan for 30 seconds.
6. Finally, add the ground oregano and French fries, tossing everything together for another 10 seconds to integrate all the ingredients and serve.

Pork

Stir Fried Pork with Vegetables

This one-pot meal takes only 30 minutes to prepare from start to finish and makes for a great week night dinner. Serves 4.

Ingredients:

- 1 lb. lean pork, cubed
- 10 oz cut green beans
- 2 large yellow onions, sliced
- 1 green pepper, sliced
- 1 red bell pepper, sliced
- 2 Tbsp of butter
- 1 tsp salt
- ½ tsp paprika
- ½ tsp black pepper
- 1 ½ cups chicken broth
- 4 Tbsp of ketchup
- 2 Tbsp of cornstarch
- Jasmine rice

Directions:

1. Add onions and peppers to butter in a wok or large skillet. Sauté for 1 minute. Add the green beans and the pork, and stir-fry over high heat until the pork is cooked through. Add salt, paprika, and black pepper. Mix well.
2. Pour in the chicken broth, cover, and simmer for 15 minutes or until vegetables are al dente.
3. Mix the ketchup with the cornstarch. Stir the mixture into the pan or wok. Cook, stirring, until the juices are thickened.
4. Prepare the jasmine rice.

Serve the stir-fry over the rice and enjoy!

Stuffed Pork Chops

Ingredients:
- 3 Tbsp butter
- 1 cup fresh mushrooms, chopped
- 1 cup seasoned cornbread stuffing (make this according to the directions on the package)
- 3 Tbsp chicken broth
- 1 cup shredded white cheddar cheese, 4 oz
- 3 tsp chopped fresh sage leaves (or dried)
- 6 bone-in pork loin chops, 1 inch thick about 4 pounds, trimmed of fat
- ¼ tsp salt
- ¼ teaspoon freshly ground pepper
- 1 Tbsp olive oil

Directions:
1. Pre-heat oven to 350°F. In a 12-inch nonstick skillet, melt 1 Tbsp of butter over med-high heat.
2. Cook mushrooms in butter 2-3 minutes or until tender Remove from heat, add stuffing and broth, stir until liquid is absorbed. Stir in cheese and 2 tsp of the sage.
3. Prepare the cornbread stuffing according to the directions on the package.
4. Make a pocket in each pork chop by cutting into the side of the chop toward the bone. Spoon stuffing mixture into each pocket, secure opening with toothpicks. Sprinkle pork with salt, pepper and remaining 1 teaspoon of sage.
5. In the same skillet melt remaining 2 Tbsp butter over med-high heat. Add 3 pork chops, cook 4 minutes, turning once until brown.
6. Spray broiler pan rack with cooking spray. Place pork on rack in pan. Repeat with remaining pork chops. Brush pork chops with oil. Bake 20 minutes or until the thermometer inserted in center of meat portion reads 145°F. (Or bake in air fryer.)

Let stand 3 minutes and serve.

Crockpot Pork Tenderloin

This is a classic at my mom's house. She's a self-identified meat and potatoes kind of gal and has perfected this savory recipe. Serves 4.

Ingredients:

- 2/3 cup dry white wine, such as Pinot Grigio
- 2 Tbsp light soy sauce
- 2 tsp granulated sugar
- 1 large clove garlic, crushed
- 1 1/4 pounds whole pork tenderloin
- 2 tsp extra virgin olive oil
- 1/4 stick of butter
- 3 potatoes (your choice)
- 1/2 bag baby carrots
- 3-4 stalks of celery
- 1/2 white onion
- Salt and pepper to taste

Directions:

1. In a small bowl combine all ingredients except meat and oil, stir to dissolve sugar. Cut tenderloin crosswise into 10-12 slices about 1 inch thick.
2. Place tenderloin in bowl and seal marinate 15-20 minutes. Place marinade, one cup of water, meat and veggies into crockpot on high heat for 90 minutes, then reduce to low heat for 30 minutes. The pork should reach an internal temperature of 165°F.
3. Serve once meat is cooked through and veggies are tender.

*If you're short on time, you can buy a Hormel brand pre-marinated pork tenderloin in the meat section of your local grocery store, toss it in the crockpot with some potatoes, carrots, or celery then set it, and forget it.

Fish

Richard's Salmon Croquettes

Ingredients:

- 14 oz canned pink salmon (Remove any bone or skin, squeeze out oil.) Reserve the salmon oil to add in later if final mix is too dry.
- 1/3 cup onions, diced
- 1/4 cup bell pepper, diced (your choice of color)
- 1 tsp creole seasoning (can sub for magic seafood blend)
- 1 Tbsp old bay seasoning, optional
- 1 Tbsp garlic powder
- 2 Tbsp parsley flakes
- 1/2 tsp black pepper
- 1/2 tsp cayenne pepper (optional)
- 1/4 cup flour
- 1/4 cup cornmeal (can sub for breadcrumbs or even well diced bread)
- 1 egg, slightly beaten
- 3 Tbsp mayonnaise

Tartar sauce:
2 cups of mayonnaise, 2 Tbsp lemon juice, pinches of; of lemon pepper, dill weed, and salt. Adjust to your taste. (In a hurry? Grab a bottle of craft brand tartar sauce at the store and add lemon juice and fresh cracked pepper to brighten it up.)

Directions:

1. Mix well, make patties to desired size. Add saved salmon oil if your mixture is too dry, add flour if too wet.
2. Refrigerate for 45 minutes minimum. This helps prevent breaking when handling and flipping.
3. Make the tartar sauce.
4. Place patties in an air fryer basket, spray the top of patties with cooking oil. Set air fryer to 380°F for 10 minutes. Check after 6-8 minutes.
5. Flip all patties. Spray with light cooking oil and set air fryer to 400°F for 4 minutes. Check after 2 minutes. Serve with a dollop of tartar sauce.

White Fish with Cherry Tomatoes and Balsamic

I love making this easy dish during weeknights when I have less time than on the weekends. It only takes 20 minutes to prepare and serves 4.

Ingredients:
- 6 Tbsp olive oil, divided
- (4) 6 oz white fish fillets, skinned
- 1/2 tsp salt, divided
- 1/4 tsp freshly ground black pepper
- 2 cups cherry tomatoes
- 3 garlic cloves, minced
- 2 Tbsp balsamic vinegar
- 2 Tbsp chopped fresh basil

Directions:
1. Heat a large nonstick skillet over medium heat, add 3 Tbsp olive oil. Sprinkle fish fillets with a quarter tsp of salt and pepper. Add fish to pan, cook 5 minutes on each side or until fish flakes easily when tested with a fork. Remove fish from pan. Keep warm.
2. Add remaining 3 Tbsp of oil to pan. Add tomatoes and garlic, sauté 3 minutes. Add balsamic vinegar and cook 1 minute or until tomatoes begin to burst.
3. Stir in basil and remaining 1/4 tsp salt. Serve tomato mixture with fish.

You can serve this dish with a side of noodles or rice, or even mashed potatoes.

Pastas

Mediterranean Orzo Pasta

This is a very quick pasta to put together. And you can add protein such as chicken to make it a complete meal. Total time: 20 minutes. Serves 6. Serve chilled.

Ingredients:
- 1 ½ cup of dry orzo pasta
- 1 pint of cherry tomatoes, cut in half
- 2 green onions, trimmed and chopped (white and green parts)
- 1/2 green bell pepper seeds removed, chopped
- 1 cup packed chopped fresh parsley
- 1/2 cup packed chopped fresh dill
- 1/4 cup sliced pitted Kalamata olives
- 2 tsp capers
- Feta cheese, to your liking.

Dressing:
- 1 lemon's zest and juice, 1/4 cup olive oil, one garlic clove, minced 1 tsp oregano. Mix together.

Directions:
1. Cook the orzo pasta according to package instructions. Drain and cool in fridge.
2. In a large bowl, combine cherry tomatoes, green onions, bell peppers, parsley, dill, olives, and capers, then add the orzo pasta (it's ok if it's still a little warm).
3. Make your dressing. In a small bowl, combine the lemon juice, lemon zest, olive oil, garlic, oregano, and a decent pinch of salt and black pepper. Whisk to combine.
4. Pour the dressing over the salad and toss until combined and the orzo pasta is well coated with the dressing. Top with pieces of feta cheese. Cover and refrigerate until it's cold before serving.

Penne Pasta with Salmon and Asparagus in Light Cream Sauce

Ingredients:

- ½ cup olive oil, and 2 Tbsp of olive oil
- 1 cup uncooked penne pasta
- 1/2 tsp white pepper
- 1/2 tsp dried dillweed
- 1/2 tsp salt
- 1 1/2 pounds of salmon fillet (enough for 4 servings)
- 1 cup fresh asparagus cut into 1-inch pieces (steam the thick pieces only)
- 4 cloves of garlic
- 4 slices, fresh lemon
- 3 cups heavy cream
- 1/2 cup freshly grated Parmesan cheese
- 2 pinches of salt

Directions:

1. Fill a large pot with salted water, boil. Pour in 2 Tbsp of olive oil, stirring penne and return to boil cook uncovered occasionally until al dente about 11 minutes. Drain well.
2. Heat 1/2 cup olive oil, white pepper, dill and ½ tsp of salt in a skillet over medium-low heat until the oil is simmering. Lay salmon fillets into the oil and sprinkle with 2 pinches of salt.
3. Arrange cut asparagus and bits of minced garlic around the salmon in the skillet. Squeeze the lemon slices over it all and place the squeezed slices into the skillet.
4. Cover and cook for 8 minutes. Flip the salmon and cook 8 more minutes until the salmon is done. Remove the salmon, asparagus, garlic, and lemon slices from the skillet to a plate, leaving the juices in the skillet.
5. Whisk in the cream and enough parmesan cheese to thicken the sauce. Let the cheese melt and season to taste with salt.
6. Spoon the cream sauce over the pasta and serve!

Mom's Pasta Salad

My mom made this pasta on weeknights when I was growing up, and now I make it for my family when time is in short supply. Bursting with flavor, this pasta has it all, protein, veggies, and great taste! Serve chilled.

Ingredients:
- 1 box of tri-color rotini pasta
- 1 salami (cubed)
- ½ block cheddar cheese, cubed
- 2-3 cups broccoli florets, raw, chopped well
- 1/2 lemon
- 1 bottle Cheese Fantastico Dressing, light (Bernstein's brand)

Directions:
1. Cook the pasta on the stovetop, drain, and set aside to cool.
2. Cube the salami and cheese.
3. Chop the broccoli florets.
4. Add broccoli, salami, and dressing (to taste) to pasta.
5. Add ½ of the lemon juice to the mixture (lemon juice really brightens a pasta dish!)
6. Put in the fridge to chill 20-30 minutes.

Once chilled, add the cheese and serve!

Vegetarian & Vegan

Eggplant Parmesan

Ingredients:
- 2/3 cup breadcrumbs
- 1 Tbsp and ¼ cup Parmesan cheese, grated
- 1/2 clove of garlic, pressed
- 1/2 tsp thyme
- 1/2 tsp oregano
- 1 medium eggplant (about 1 1/2 pounds)
- 2 1/2 cups of tomato sauce
- 1/2 cup basil
- 4 oz shredded mozzarella cheese

Directions:
1. In a mixing bowl, combine breadcrumbs, Parmesan cheese, thyme, and oregano.
2. Cut eggplant into (8) 2-inch slices and place into a 9"x13" greased baking pan. Cover with breadcrumbs. Bake at 400° F for 20-25 minutes.
3. Combine tomato sauce, Parmesan cheese and basil. Pour over eggplant. Sprinkle with grated cheese, bake for 15 more minutes.
4. Cut, serve, and buen provecho!

Spicy Zucchini Taco Boats

This vegetarian recipe calls for impossible ground beef or beyond beef but could easily be made for meat lovers using ground beef or even lean ground turkey. Busy day ahead of you? You can also prepare this dish in advance by assembling your zucchini boats earlier in the day, then storing them covered in the fridge until you're ready to bake.

Ingredients:

- 4 large zucchinis, cut in half lengthwise and seeded
- 2 cups spicy salsa (or salsa of choice)
- 1 pound of meat (impossible ground beef, or your choice)
- 1 oz taco seasoning packet
- 1 tsp garlic powder
- 1/2 tsp each; cumin, chili powder, paprika
- 1/2 a small yellow onion, minced
- 1 large red bell pepper, diced
- 1 (18 oz) can of tomato sauce
- 1 small jalapeño
- 1 tsp red pepper chili flakes
- 1/4 cup water
- 1/2 cup shredded cheese (my family likes the Mexican blend)

Optional toppings:
1 medium avocado cubed, 1/4 cup chopped scallions, 1/2 cup cherry tomatoes, parsley for garnish.

Directions:
1. Preheat oven to 400°F. Place 1 cup of spicy salsa on the bottom of a 9"x13" baking dish.
2. Blanche the zucchini halves by bringing a large pot of salted water to boil and placing the zucchini, seeds removed, in the boiling water for 1-2 minutes. Drain and set the halves in the prepared baking dish.
3. Cook the ground meat over medium heat in a large skillet. When meat is almost fully cooked, add the taco seasoning, spices, onion, jalapeño, bell pepper, salsa, tomato sauce, and water and mix well. Let this come to a simmer and cook 2-3 minutes more.
4. Using a spoon, fill the hollowed zucchini boats with the meat, dividing the taco meat equally. Sprinkle cheese on top. Cover loosely with foil and bake for 10-15 minutes or until zucchini is cooked through.

Soups & Stews

French Onion Soup

I know this is wildly cliché, but I first tried French onion soup in France. After that I spent a number of years looking into and testing out the perfect, simple recipe for this amazing classic.
Cooking time: 1 hour and 10 minutes total. Yields 4 - 6 servings.

Ingredients:
- 1/2 cup unsalted butter
- 2 garlic cloves, pressed
- 2 bay leaves, chopped
- 2 sprigs fresh thyme
- Salt and freshly ground black pepper
- ½ a bottle of red wine (I like to use a Merlot or a red blend)
- 3 heaping Tbsp all-purpose flour
- 2 quarts beef broth
- 1 baguette, sliced
- 1/2 pound grated Gruyere cheese

Directions:
1. Melt the stick of butter in a large pot over medium heat. Add the onions, garlic, bay leaves, thyme, and salt and pepper and cook until the onions are very soft and caramelized, about 25 minutes. Add the wine, bring to a boil, then reduce the heat and simmer until the wine has evaporated and the onions are dry, about 5 minutes. Discard the bay leaves and thyme sprigs. Dust the onions with the flour and stir them gently.
2. Turn the heat down to medium low (so the flower doesn't burn) and cook for approximately 10 minutes more. Add the beef broth and bring the soup back to a simmer and cook for 10 more minutes. Season to taste with salt and pepper.
3. Pre-heat the broiler (or use your airfryer) and arrange the baguette slices on a baking sheet in a single layer. Lightly butter and salt them, then sprinkle the slices with the Gruyere cheese and broil until bubbly and golden brown, about 3 - 5 minutes.
4. Ladle soup into bowls and place on top. Voilà!

(A more time consuming but more authentic alternative is to ladle the soup into bowls, top each with a slice of bread and cheese, then put the bowls into the oven to toast the bread and melt the cheese.)

Butternut Squash Soup

Ingredients:
- 1 ½ Tbsp butter
- ½ yellow onion, sliced
- 2 cloves garlic
- 2 sprigs fresh thyme
- ½ butternut squash, peeled, seeded, and cut into 1-inch cubes
- 4 cups chicken broth
- ½ cube chicken bouillon
- 1 pinch ground cumin
- 1 pinch ground allspice
- Salt and ground black pepper, to taste

Directions:
1. Melt butter in a large pot over medium heat. Add onion, garlic, and thyme and sauté until onion has softened, about 5 minutes. Add squash and chicken broth; bring to a simmer, then cook until squash is tender, 10-15 minutes.
2. Crumble bouillon into the soup. Season with cumin, allspice, salt, and pepper, then remove from heat.
3. Working in batches, pour soup into a blender, filling no more than halfway. Hold the lid in place with a kitchen towel, then carefully start the blender using a few quick pulses to get the soup moving before leaving it on to purée. Alternately, you can use a stick blender and purée the soup.
4. Pour soup into a soup tureen and serve up!

Weeknight Taco Soup

This is an awesome one pot solution that is guaranteed to please the whole family! Total time 30 minutes. Yields 4-6 servings or 2 1/2 quarts.

Ingredients:
- 1 Tbsp avocado oil
- 1 large, white onion, chopped
- 1 lb lean ground hamburger meat
- 1 medium, sweet red pepper, chopped
- 1 medium green pepper, chopped
- 1can (28 oz) diced tomatoes undrained
- 3 cups vegetable broth
- 1 can (15 oz) pinto beans, rinsed and drained
- 1 ½ cups corn
- 1 envelope of taco seasoning
- 1/4 tsp salt
- 1/4 tsp pepper
- 1 package (8.8 oz) ready-to-serve long grain rice
- 1 cup sour cream

Optional toppings;
Shredded cheddar cheese, crushed tortilla chips, and additional sour cream.

Directions:
1. In a Dutch oven or big stew pot, heat oil over medium heat. Add onion and peppers. Cook until crisp-tender 3-5 minutes.
2. Add tomatoes, broth, beans, corn, taco seasoning, salt, and pepper, bring to a boil.
3. Reduce heat and simmer uncovered until veggies are tender, 10-15 minutes. Reduce heat, stirring rice and sour cream. Heat through.

Serve with toppings. This recipe will also freeze beautifully in a freezer container.

Desserts

"Oh taste and see that the Lord is good; blessed is the man who takes refuge in him."
Psalm 34:8

I think a dessert completes dinnertime. There's something so satisfying about being able to whip out a glorious confection after you've just served a sublime meal. To quote my grandfather, Papa, we have a "sweet tooth" at Casa de Romero. As a grandfather should, my Papa taught me many things about life. He was born in 1923 and lived until almost 97 years of age, having served this great nation as an active combat marine in WWII. I am so proud of him, the ancestor of pilgrims to New England and a descendant of hardworking farmers who kissed the ground of this country upon arrival, the youngest of eight children, and the tremendous effort and trauma he went through to alleviate the world of the Nazi regime. A man of God, a family man, and a sweetheart, now in glory with our Lord, he taught me the value of a "sampler platter" when it came to desserts. Papa, this chapter is for you.

Easy Cinnamon Baked Apples

We have an apple tree in our backyard, so I have spent years exploring baked apple recipes. This one is a tried-and-true delight for my family and friends. It serves 6, is fridge friendly for 3-4 days, and freezer friendly for 1 month.

Ingredients:

- 6-7 medium to large apples. (If buying your apples from the grocery store, you can mix 2 tarts such as Granny Smith, and 4 sweets such as Honey Crisp.)
- 2 Tbsp lemon juice
- 1 Tbsp coconut oil (optional)
- 2/3 cup cane sugar (can substitute up to half of sugar with Stevia)
- 1 1/2 tsp ground cinnamon
- 3/4 tsp ginger
- 3 Tbsp cornstarch for thickening the sauce
- 3 Tbsp of fresh apple juice (can substitute with water)
- A pinch of nutmeg
- A pinch of sea salt

Directions:

1. Preheat your oven to 350°F and set out a 9"x13" or similar size baking dish.
2. Peel and core the apples, quarter, and use a paring knife to thinly slice lengthwise, the thinner the better. Just try to be consistent so they cook evenly.
3. Add to baking dish and top with lemon juice, coconut oil, optional cane sugar, cinnamon, ginger, nutmeg, cornstarch, apple juice, or water, and a healthy pinch of salt, tossed to combine then loosely cover with foil.
4. Bake for 45 minutes covered, then carefully remove foil and bake for an additional 10-15 minutes or until the apples are very fork tender, especially in the center of the dish, and slightly caramelized. Add a bit of water if the caramel "sauce" is too thick.

*Enjoy as-is or with whipped cream and/or a la mode with vanilla bean ice cream. You can also crumble some granola on top.

Pies

Blueberry Cream Pie

There is something that feels so Americana about having blueberry pie in the summer. I usually make this pie and take it along for Independence Day. Delicious blueberries, fireworks, kids, splashing in the pool. God is good. You can either buy a prepared piecrust, or if you have extra time on your hands, use the following recipe to create your crust.

Pie Crust Ingredients:
- 1 stick of butter
- 1 cup of flour
- 1/4 cup of brown sugar
- 3/4 cup slivered almonds

Directions:
1. Cream sugar and butter.
2. Add in flour and nuts. Press into (2) 10-inch pie tins.
3. Bake at 375°F 10-15 minutes.

For the filling (base layer):
- 8 ounces of cream cheese
- 3/4 cup packed granulated sugar
- 1 tsp vanilla extract
- 2 tubs of Cool Whip
- Mix these all together in a bowl

Topping: 1 can of blueberry pie filling

Directions:
1. Bake crust according to the instructions. Let it cool.
2. Pour the filling over the baked crust. Chill for at least 3 hours.
4. Then pour the topping over the filling and chill.
5. Serve with vanilla ice cream on the side. Enjoy!

Pecan Pie

Ingredients:
- 3 eggs, well beaten
- 1 Tbsp butter
- 1 cup brown sugar
- 1 cup karo syrup
- 1 cup pecans
- 1 tsp vanilla extract
- Pinch of salt

Directions:
1. Cream butter and sugar. Add syrup, well beaten eggs, salt and vanilla. Add nuts.
2. Turn into an uncooked pie shell.
3. Bake at 350°F for about 1 hour or until the center is set.

Muffins

Banana Sour Cream Muffins

Moist, tender, and just the right amount of sweet, these muffins are a comforting treat perfect for breakfast or tea. The sour cream adds richness and depth, making each bite soft, flavorful, and utterly satisfying. Yields: 4 dozen.

Ingredients:
- 1 cup sugar
- 1 1/2 cups flour
- 1 tsp baking soda
- 1/2 tsp salt
- 2 eggs
- 1/2 cup vegetable oil
- 1/2 cup non-fat sour cream
- 1 tsp vanilla extract
- 2 ripe bananas, mashed (1 cup)
- Paper cups for muffin tin

Directions:
1. Mix all the ingredients together in a bowl.
2. Pour into lined muffin tins.
3. Bake at 350°F for 20 mins.
4. Enjoy hot with some melted butter on top!

Bran Muffins

Hearty, nourishing, and subtly sweet, these classic bran muffins are a feel-good favorite packed with fiber and flavor. Perfect with a pat of butter or a drizzle of honey, they're a wholesome way to start the day- or enjoy as a snack any time. This batter will keep up to 3 months if stored in a plastic or glass container with a tight lid in the fridge.

Ingredients:
- 1 box of raisin bran (16 oz)
- 1 cup of raisins
- 3 cups of granulated sugar
- 5 cups of all-purpose flour
- 5 tsp of baking soda
- 1 tsp of salt
- 4 eggs
- 1 cup of vegetable oil
- 1 quart of buttermilk
- Paper cups for muffin tin

Directions:
1. In a large, non-metal mixing bowl, mix the dry ingredients then the eggs, oil and buttermilk. Add 1 cup of raisins for extra sweetness.
2. Once ingredients are combined, do not stir anymore. Using a 1/3 cup measuring cup, pour the batter into paper cups in a muffin tin.
3. Bake at 400°F for 15-20 minutes.

Cookies

Cookies can be a little tricky due to their shallow and small surface area. Here are some tips and tricks you can use when baking cookies. If your cookies are crumbly, substitute bread flour for some of the all-purpose flour and add a few drops of water. The higher protein content of bread flour will create more gluten and make the cookies chewier. For flat and thin cookies, substitute shortening for part of the butter. Because of its higher melting temperature, shortening gives cookies more time to set and stay domed. Also, chill the dough before it goes in the oven. Additionally, a dash of cream of tartar powder will help make cookies fluffy. If your cookies are too pale, substitute 2 tablespoons of corn syrup for an equal amount of sugar, as it browns at a lower temperature. You can also utilize dark brown sugar to help obtain a more golden-brown look.

Cookies will freeze beautifully, which is a saving grace when you're short on time but have the opportunity to get all your Christmas cookies done at once. Wrap cookies, individually, or in pairs back-to-back in plastic wrap. It takes only a few minutes to wrap cookies this way and they keep much better than if they are just tossed into a freezer bag. Bar cookies and brownies should be wrapped in plastic and then a double layer of aluminum foil. Sticky or frosted cookies or bars should be frozen unwrapped first just long enough to firm up their tops. Label cookie storage containers or bags with a piece of masking tape, indicating the type of cookie and the date they were frozen. Cookies can be frozen for up to 90 days. After that, their taste and texture will start to deteriorate. To defrost, let cookies defrost in their wrapping so that any moisture that forms will stay on the wrapping, not the cookies. If the weather is very humid, don't let crisp cookies stand out for too long, or they will begin to lose their texture. If you encounter stale cookies, toss a piece of bread in the bag, and your cookies will come back to life.

Oatmeal Chocolate Chip Cookies

My maternal grandmother had family on the Eastern seaboard of Canada in Nova Scotia. This was a family recipe passed down, and I used to make it in the kitchen with both my Nana and my mother growing up, and now I make it with my children. Prep time: 15 minutes. Bake time: 10 minutes. Yields approximately 4 dozen.

Ingredients:
- 2 sticks of butter
- 1 cup granulated sugar
- 1/2 cup of brown sugar
- 2 eggs
- 2 1/2 cups flour sifted, (be generous)
- 3/4 tsp baking soda
- 2 cups old-fashioned oatmeal
- 1 tsp vanilla extract
- 1 cup chocolate chips (Nestlé semi sweet)

Directions:
1. Mix wet ingredients.
2. Add dry ingredients.
3. Bake at 350°F for 10 minutes.

Great Grandma's Applesauce Drop Cookies

I love this recipe. Not only because it was handed down in my family and is also delicious, but because I often have extra applesauce lying around too.

Ingredients:

- 1/2 cup butter
- 1 1/4 cup granulated sugar
- 1 egg
- 1 1/4 cup applesauce
- 1 cup raisins
- 1/2 cup chopped nuts (your preference)
- 2 1/2 cups flour
- 1 tsp baking soda
- 1 tsp cinnamon
- 1/4 tsp cloves
- 1 tsp salt

Directions:

1. Sift the flower once, then sift it again with the other dry ingredients.
2. Cream the butter and sugar. Add eggs and mix well.
3. Mix dry ingredients alternately with applesauce.
4. Bake at 375°F for 10 minutes.

Bon appétit!

Snickerdoodle Cookies

This was my Nana's recipe, and growing up, I'd smell it in her kitchen before I even walked through the door. It was one of her go-to cookies. They're so delicious.
Yield: 3 dozen.

Ingredients:
- 1 cup butter
- 1 ½ cups granulated sugar plus 2 Tbsp sugar
- 2 eggs
- 2 3/4 cups flour
- 2 tsp cream of tartar
- 1 tsp baking soda
- 1/2 tsp salt
- 2 Tbsp cinnamon

Directions:
1. Cream together butter and sugar. Add eggs, mix well.
2. Sift together remaining dry ingredients and add to creamed mixture and mix well.
3. Chill dough. Shape into balls the size of walnuts, roll in sugar and cinnamon mixture, which is 2 Tbsp cinnamon and 2 Tbsp granulated sugar, and place on an ungreased cookie sheet.
4. Bake at 400°F for 8-10 minutes, or until lightly browned but still soft. Cookies will puff up and then flatten while baking.

Brownies

Ingredients:
- 2 cups granulated sugar
- 2 sticks of butter, melted and cooled
- 4 eggs
- A dash of salt
- 2 cups flour
- 3 Tbsp unsweetened cocoa
- 2 Tbsp vanilla extract

Chocolate glaze:
- 3 Tbsp melted butter
- 1 Tbsp cocoa
- 3 Tbsp milk
- 1 tsp vanilla extract

Mix the melted butter and cocoa together, then add the milk and vanilla.

Directions:
1. Mix flour, sugar, salt, and cocoa together.
2. Add melted butter, eggs, vanilla, and mix. Add pecans and stir (optional).
3. Pour into a 14"x10" pan and bake at 350°F for 25 minutes.

Note: you can add some powdered sugar if you'd like to thicken your glaze, but it shouldn't be too thick (such as a frosting). Pour the glaze over the brownies while they're still hot.
Cut into squares and serve!

Cakes

Ah, cake. My favorite dessert, hands down. A relatively little-known fact about me is that in college I was interning at a big fashion company and making peanuts, so I started a bespoke cake bakery out of my home kitchen to earn a little extra cash. I think cake is one of life's greatest pleasures. Think about it, it's bread, and sweet, and there are so many flavor combinations you can create, not to mention the endless ways of presentation and design.

I love every aspect of baking and decorating a cake. From the sweet aroma wafting up from my Kitchen Aid mixer to leveling off the tops (and letting my kids eat them), to stacking the cake in what can only be described as an architectural marvel, then decorating the cake to your heart's delight. I've learned that when decorating cakes, a little frosting covers a multitude of sins, and more is better.

Mid-Century Chocolate Cake

Everyone in my family loves chocolate cake! So I find myself making plenty of chocolate cakes each year. This recipe is for a large cake, suitable for serving a gathering of 10-12 people.

Ingredients:
- 3 cups sifted cake flour
- 2 cups white granulated sugar
- 1 cup ground chocolate
- 1 cup of vegetable oil
- 2 eggs
- 1 cup of buttermilk
- 2 tsp baking soda
- 1 tsp vanilla extract
- 1 cup boiling water

Directions:
1. Add ingredients to the bowl in the order given.
2. Mix 3-4 minutes until all ingredients are well incorporated.
3. Bake in oven at 350°F for 45 minutes or until the cake springs back when lightly touched with finger.

Strawberry Trifle with Poundcake

This trifle is a crowd pleaser no matter where I take it and just about every time I make it, someone asks me for the recipe. This recipe is written using a poundcake bought from the bakery, which is what I often must use to save time. However, if you're not pressed for time, see Grandma's Buttermilk Poundcake recipe immediately after this one and make the pound cake.

Ingredients:
- 2 lbs fresh strawberries, sliced
- 16 oz container of pound cake, cubed
- 1 package of instant vanilla pudding (5.1 oz size) (You can opt for the sugar-free version.)
- 3 cups of milk for the pudding
- 8 ounce tub of Cool Whip (I get reduced fat)
- 1/2 cup of sugar (you can use Truvia or Splenda for baking)

Directions:
1. Add the sugar to the strawberries and toss to coat. Set aside in the fridge for 30 minutes for them to gel, tossing at least 1-2 more times.
2. Prepare the pudding as directed. Gently fold in Cool Whip. Set aside in the fridge till needed.
3. Layer your ingredients into the trifle bowl in this order: 1/3 of the pound cake, 1/3 of the pudding mixture, and then 2/5 of the strawberries.
4. Repeat these layers twice more. The final layer of strawberries should be slightly less than 1/5 versus the 2/5 used in earlier layers.

Refrigerate the trifle for at least 2 hours before serving. Enjoy!

Grandma's Buttermilk Poundcake

Ingredients:
- 2 sticks of butter
- 3 cups granulated sugar
- 5 eggs
- 3 cups flour
- 1/4 tsp salt
- 1/2 tsp baking soda
- 1 cup buttermilk
- 1 tsp vanilla extract
- 1/2 tsp almond extract (or extract of your choosing)

Directions:
1. Grease and flour a tube pan.
2. Cream together butter and sugar, beat in eggs, one at a time. Soften together with the dry ingredients and add buttermilk. Add an extract in flavor of your choice (optional).
3. Bake at 325°F for 1 1/2 hours. (Adaptation: use sour cream instead of buttermilk and add an extra egg.)
4. Take the cake out of the pan and allow to cool on racks.

Cut and serve with coffee, or with fresh berries and whipped cream.

Old Fashioned Crumb Cake

Ingredients:
- 1 cup vegetable shortening (such as Crisco)
- 2 cups of brown sugar
- 2 cups flour, sifted
- 1 Tbsp salt
- 1 slightly beaten egg
- 1 cup buttermilk
- 1 tsp cinnamon
- 1 tsp vanilla extract
- 1 tsp baking soda
- 1/2 cups crushed nuts (your choice)

Directions:
1. Cream shortening, brown sugar, flour and salt. Take out 1 cup of the mixture and set aside for topping the rest of the mixture.
2. Then add the egg, buttermilk, vanilla extract, and baking soda. Mix well.
3. Pour into a 9"x12" greased pan.
4. To the cup of crumb mixture, add cinnamon and nuts. Stir, and sprinkle over batter in pan.
5. Bake in a 350°F oven for about 30-35 minutes.

Welcome Home: *A Guide to Homemaking From the Heart*

Cupcakes

"So whether you eat or drink, or whatever you do, do it all for the glory of God."
1 Corinthians 10:31

Cupcakes. One would think that because I love cakes and cake decorating so much, and even crafted a small business out of it, that I would similarly be enamored by cupcakes. Not true. At the risk of getting my spatula taken away from me, I'd say that cupcakes are a necessity, not a decadent luxury. No offense to my cupcake lovers, I realize plenty of brides in recent years have opted for cupcake towers and spreads at their weddings. At the same time, with cupcakes, your wedding coordinator or baker doesn't need to hand cut and serve the slices- guests may simply grab and go, hence a necessity.

Cupcakes have a time and a place- I always make cupcakes for my children's class parties at school. (To me, buying store bought just doesn't demonstrate my way of showing thoughtfulness, care and love. Not that homemade is the only way to do this!) There have been times where I have been much too busy with work, or submitting our taxes, or Doctor appointments, and I have to cut corners. In those cases, I have purchased store bought cupcakes to save on the time of baking. And honestly, the price is the same, if not even cheaper nowadays, due to big box stores' ability to create economies of scale with their baked goods. I scrape off all the frosting, put on some jazz music, light a candle, and get swept up in the joy of decorating the cupcakes myself.

In my more stressed times, I've asked myself, "Do these kids even care?!" To which I have reflected, and answered from my heart in a small voice, "But *I* care". And there you have it. Making the cupcakes myself doesn't just represent a cute cupcake that will delight children and be demolished in three bites. It represents celebrating a holiday or life event, building memories, having beautiful pictures to look back on, hearing squeals of joy when they see something unique, creative, and made just for them. Not to mention the mom credit when they say with bewilderment, "*Your mom made these*?!" It's not about the accolades to me, although I'd be lying if I said they weren't a delightful little perk, it's about loving on my children in my way, and making them proud of me. I am so proud of them. I have beautiful, kind, loving, amazing children, and I am so blessed. I want to reflect that back to them.

Orange Streusel Cake

Short on time but still want to bring something homemade? This tasty orange streusel cake is just what you need!

Ingredients:
- 1 box orange cake mix (Duncan Hines). (Include the ingredients from the package.)
- 1 package of instant vanilla pudding (3.4 oz)

For the streusel:
- Mix 1/2 cup flour
- 1/2 cup of brown sugar
- 1 tsp cinnamon
- 3 Tbsp melted butter

Optional glaze:
- 1 ¼ cup powdered sugar
- 2 Tbsp orange juice
- 4 Tbsp melted butter

Directions:
1. Mix cake mix and all the ingredients together, beating well.
2. In a separate bowl, mix the streusel.
3. Spray a cupcake tin with cooking spray.
4. In each cupcake cup, fill ½ the cup with batter, then sprinkle 2 Tbsp of streusel on top, then add 1 spoonful of batter on top. Finally, sprinkle streusel on top.
5. Bake about 45-50 minutes at 375°F.
6. Prepare the glaze and drizzle over cooled cupcakes or frost with the cream cheese frosting recipe on the next page.

Enjoy!

Cream Cheese Frosting

I have made and tried tons of frostings in my time, and I can honestly say that this frosting is one of the best I have ever had. It is my sincere pleasure to share it with you because while you may think it's impossible to mess up something as wonderful and sweet as frosting, the reality is that not all frostings are the same. Some are too greasy, some are too loose, so when you just want an old school frosting that tastes like heaven, this one's for you. This frosting has a cream cheese base and will cover a 2-layer 9-inch cake or 24 cupcakes.

Ingredients:
- 1 ½ cups unsalted butter, softened and cut into pieces
- 8 oz cream cheese, softened and cut into pieces
- 4 cups of powdered sugar (can substitute Truvia, a sugar-free powdered sugar for baking) sift your powdered sugar, do not skip this step
- 1 Tbsp vanilla extract
- 1/8 tsp salt
- Dash of white food dye (optional to crisp up the white color)

Directions:
1. Place butter into a large mixing bowl with an electric mixer. Beat until smooth and creamy, then beat on high speed 1 minute until lightened in color, (the longer you beat the lighter the color will become).
2. Beat and soften cream cheese just until combined, scraping down the bowl.
3. Beat in vanilla and salt until incorporated, sifted powdered sugar, one cup at a time and mix on low speed until incorporated. Once all of the powdered sugar is in, increase to high speed and beat another 2-3 minutes until whipped, thick and spreadable, scraping down the bowl a couple of times to ensure everything is really well blended.

*A note on store-bought frosting…if I'm pressed for time, I'll get store bought (zero sugar) frosting to do my crumb coat on a cake. You can expand a container of store bought frosting by whipping it with your mixer for a few minutes and you can actually double it in size. Because it's aerated, you'll get to frost more cake or cupcakes with the same amount, and the amount of sugar and calories per serving is reduced.

Beverages

"But whoever drinks the water I give them will never thirst. Indeed, the water I give them will become in them a spring of water welling up to eternal life." John 4:14

I am such a big fan of infused water. It's a great way to take something that is simple and elevate it. I don't drink wine except for social occasions, but I do miss at times the experience of holding the glass so I will put my infused water into a crystal wine glass for a touch of sophistication and self-care at home. Always wash your produce first, and serve waters chilled. For optimal freshness, drink within 24 hours.

Fresh Lemon and English Cucumber Water

Slice 1/2 of a cucumber and 1 lemon. Add to water in a pitcher. Optional: garnish with mint. Chill for at least 20 minutes and enjoy over ice.

Bright Orange and Luscious Blueberry Water

Mix about 20 blueberries, 1 sliced orange (of any variety), and water in a pitcher.
Chill for at least 20 minutes, pour over ice, and enjoy!

Tangy Cranberry and Lime Fizz

I love this recipe for parties. Both children and adults love it, and it's much healthier than even a diet soda, but refreshing and hydrating, too.

Mix one jug of 100% cranberry juice (no sugar added) with 4 cups of seltzer water. Add ice. Slice a lime and squeeze juice into mixture, stir, and serve.

A Word on Alcohol

I didn't include any alcohol beverage recipes in this book, not because I dislike it, or even because I don't drink it (I will drink wine socially with friends and family), but because it's not something I wanted to write about. It's true that "It is for freedom that Christ has set us free, and at the same time we are called to stand firm and not let ourselves be burdened by a yoke of slavery" (Galatians 5:1). Additionally, we're told in 1 Corinthians 10:23 "All things are lawful for me, but not all things are helpful; all things are lawful for me, but not all things edify." And finally, Paul, our Godfather of the faith, outlines for us in Romans 14:13-23:

"Therefore let us not pass judgment on one another any longer, but rather decide never to put a stumbling block or hindrance in the way of a brother. I know and am persuaded in the Lord Jesus that nothing is unclean in itself, but it is unclean for anyone who thinks it unclean. For if your brother is grieved by what you eat, you are no longer walking in love. By what you eat, do not destroy the one for whom Christ died. So do not let what you regard as good be spoken of as evil. For the Kingdom of God is not a matter of eating and drinking but of righteousness and peace and joy in the Holy Spirit. Whoever thus serves Christ is acceptable to God and approved by men. So then let us pursue what makes for peace and for mutual upbuilding. Do not, for the sake of food, destroy the work of God. Everything is indeed clean, but it is wrong for anyone to make another stumble by what he eats. It is good not to eat meat or drink wine or do anything that causes your brother to stumble. The faith that you have, keep between yourself and God. Blessed is the one who has no reason to pass judgment on himself for what he approves. But whoever has doubts is condemned if he eats, because the eating is not from faith. For whatever does not proceed from faith is sin."

Who knew food and drinks could be so controversial? The reality is that plenty of good Christian people struggle with alcohol, food, and substance dependency in various forms, so it warrants a discussion. The Enemy is a liar and a deceiver and will take the good things of God, and in the hands of mankind, twist them into vice, oppression, and tragedy. Of course, the subject of drinking wine is not the same unilaterally. What may be ok for me may not be ok for you, or what may be ok for you may not be the same for a loved one.

All this being said, we know that Jesus himself, the blameless, perfect lamb of God drank wine. We are also instructed in Ephesians 5:18, "Do not get drunk on wine, which leads to debauchery. Instead, be filled with the Spirit." In summation, the call to action is to proceed with caution.

Breads

"Man shall not live by bread alone, but by every word that comes from the mouth of God." Matthew 4:4

I couldn't possibly start talking about bread without an homage to the bread of life, Jesus Christ. As I've gotten older, I've changed my relationship with bread, being a woman who's struggled with her weight her whole life. I realize this statement applies to so many, yet I would be remiss if I didn't share that I've also struggled with eating disorders since a young age. It wasn't until I gave "my food" over to the Lord that I broke free of the bondage food had over me. And it wasn't just the food, it was the food-adjacent elements such as diets, exercise, counting calories, weighing myself and the like. I've found peace in the Lord and in moderation of His good things. Food is a good gift from God, and Jesus even likens himself to food in John 6:35. The bread of life? How do I get some of that?!

Years ago, in my travels to Europe, I would see thin women eating croissants and sipping coffee at a Parisian café. Or in Amsterdam, I'd watch as a thin woman walked away from the counter with a gorgeous pastry and I'd think, what is going on here? And don't even get me started on the dinner table outside an eatery in Italy. Hand tossed pizza, pasta puttanesca, and French bread, I can't. I believe the trick is a lifestyle that differs from ours in America- fresh, daily bread (ahem) and walking or biking as a main mode of transportation, but I digress.

I've found a few truths along the way in my life, and I wanted to share them with you. It's not a scheme to be able to eat more bread without gaining weight, I no longer think in those terms. I ask myself if this is moderation, and if I'd be able to hand over what I'm eating to the Lord. If I can say yes, then I'm likely not eating emotionally. Emotional eating to me, happens at a subconscious level wherein you're seeking to fill a void or make yourself better. And that's the crux of it. The Enemy is so crafty. He's likely not going to plant a thought in the mind of the average Christian woman to run out and have an extramarital affair. Instead, he'll distract us from living for the Lord and surrendering our will to His and tempt us to create idols- seeking satisfaction in the created, not the Creator.

"Our Father in heaven, hallowed be your name, your Kingdom come, your will be done, on earth as it is in heaven. Give us today our daily bread. And forgive us our debts, as we also have forgiven our debtors. And lead us not into temptation, but deliver us from the evil one." Matthew 6:9-13

My friend, sister in Christ, and mommy mentor to me at one of the worst times of my life as I dealt with the excruciating task of bringing home a 5-pound, oxygen-dependent, tube-fed infant, Julia Fikse, has written some wonderful, Bible-based books about food, faith and freedom (*Dear Food, I Love You, I Hate You, Don't Leave Me!*). I'm so inspired by her courage and her ministry in this area that affects so many Christian women. Her books are all available for purchase on amazon.com.

Some tried-and-true concepts I live by are;

1. Am I feeling some type of way as I reach for this?
2. Is this "worth it?" (If it's not, or the first bite doesn't delight me, I set it down.)
3. Is this fresh? Fresh bread is processed best by our bodies. After the industrial revolution, our country steered far from the farm-to-table reality, as advances in machinery and technology actually made life busier. People needed quicker, longer lasting solutions to feed their families and keep up with life's demands.

Jesus declares, "I am the bread of life. Whoever comes to me will never hunger, and whoever believes in me will never be thirsty." John 6:35

Fergasa Bread

My bestie, Courtney Ayotte, shared this recipe with me years ago. This bread is sooooo good, my family just gobbles it up!

Ingredients:
- 1-2 loaves of Bridgeford brand frozen ready dough (sold in your grocery store's freezer section)
- Extra virgin olive oil
- 1/2 white onion, sliced
- Onion powder, to taste
- Sea salt, to taste
- Fresh rosemary (optional)

Directions:
1. Take out 1-2 loaves from freezer to begin to thaw around 10am. (One loaf will feed about 6-8.)
2. Drizzle olive oil on a large or medium baking sheet with sides to keep the oil in and place the dough on top.
3. Use a basting brush to continually keep the dough wet and covered in olive oil, doing so once per hour. Once dough thaws, spread out evenly by gently kneading and stretching, but don't tear it. Let rise to fill the entire pan.
4. Keep adding olive oil to keep the dough wet. After the dough has risen (6-7 hours), place thinly sliced onions on top. I suggest using a mandolin for this. Coat again with olive oil, put onion powder on top, and lightly sprinkle sea salt. I usually put rosemary from my garden on top.
5. Set the oven at 350°F and place dough in oven until very light golden brown, approximately 20 minutes. Pull out of oven and coat heavily in olive oil and sprinkle with more sea salt.
6. Cut and serve while hot.

Cornbread

This recipe calls for coconut flour, making it a low-carb recipe. This bread takes 30 total minutes from start to finish. I usually add a little bit of date honey in my cornbread, as my family likes it a little sweeter. If your family likes a little kick, add a jalapeño to the recipe.

Ingredients:

- 6 Tbsp of butter, melted
- 1/3 cup of heavy cream
- 3 large eggs
- 1/2 cup coconut flour
- 2 Tbsp of granulated sugar (can sub for Stevia)
- 1/2 tsp salt
- 1/4 tsp baking soda
- 2 Tbsp honey (omit if a non-sweet bread is preferred)
- ½ jalapeño (optional)

Directions:

1. Preheat oven to 350°F. Spray a 10-inch cake pan or an 8"x8" baking dish with nonstick spray. Add the melted butter, cream and eggs into a mixing bowl and whisk to combine.
2. Add the coconut flour, sugar, salt and baking soda to the bowl and stir to combine. Spread the mixture into the prepared dish and bake for 15-20 minutes, or until a toothpick comes out clean.

Breakfasts

"Satisfy us in the morning with your steadfast love, that we may rejoice and be glad all our days." Psalm 90:14

Many were raised with the old adage, "Breakfast is the most important meal of the day". Well, with all due respect to the mothers that have gone before me, I'm just not a morning person. I wish I was! I often think how it would make life easier, schools start early in the morning, work beings early in the morning, and not to mention, being in Los Angeles, I wake up 3 hours behind the East Coast as it is.

Breakfast sets the tone for the day- whether it's a quiet moment with coffee and toast or a lively table full of pancakes and laughter. In this section, you'll find some of my best, most comforting and satisfying recipes to start your morning right, from slow weekend fare to quick weekday favorites.

Classic Quiche

This little gem feeds 6-8 people. I double this recipe for holidays, and we enjoy the leftovers for two days after. Prep time: 10 minutes. Bake time: 40 minutes.

Ingredients:
- 1 refrigerated pie crust, 14 oz box
- 4 large eggs
- 1 cup half-and-half
- 1 Tbsp fresh parsley, chopped, plus more for garnish
- 1 Tbsp Dijon mustard
- 1 1/2 Tbsp all-purpose flour
- 1/4 tsp kosher salt
- 8 oz package, diced ham
- 1 cup of shredded sharp cheddar cheese
- 1 small shallot, finely chopped
- 1/2 cup broccoli, chopped
- 1 cup spinach
- 1/2 cup cherry tomatoes, diced and patted dry

Directions:
1. Preheat the oven to 375°F with a baking sheet on the center rack. Fit the piecrust into a 9-inch pie plate (not a deep dish). Fold the edges of the crust under and crimp. Chill in the refrigerator while preparing the filling.
2. In a large bowl, whisk together eggs, half-and-half, parsley, mustard, flour, salt, pepper.
3. Sprinkle the ham, cheddar cheese, shallot and the rest of vegetables in the bottom of the chilled piecrust. Pour in the egg mixture.
4. Place the quiche on the preheated baking sheet and bake for 40-45 minutes until puffed up around the edges and the center is set. Let cool on the baking sheet for at least 30 minutes before slicing and serving. Garnish with fresh parsley to taste.

Cheesy Breakfast Pizza

I really like this dish because it's an all in one, featuring protein, carbs, and veggies. It's also super easy and quick to assemble.

Ingredients:

- 1 pound frozen shredded hashbrowns, defrosted
- 6 large eggs
- 6 strips bacon
- 2 cups shredded cheddar cheese
- Cherry tomatoes, quartered
- Salt and freshly ground black pepper
- Chopped fresh chives for garnish

Directions:

1. Preheat oven to 400°F. In a large mixing bowl, combine hashbrowns, 2 eggs, and 1/2 cup cheddar cheese. Season with salt and pepper.
2. Spray a pizza pan or other circular baking dish with cooking spray and add hash brown mixture. Using your hands, pat mixture into a solid circular crust. Bake 20 minutes or until golden brown.
3. Meanwhile, in a large skillet over medium heat, or in your airfryer, cook bacon until crispy (about 6 minutes). Soak up any excess grease with a paper towel.
4. Top baked crust with remaining 1 1/2 cups cheese and crack remaining 4 eggs on top. Scatter with crumbled bacon, quartered cherry tomatoes, and season all over with salt and pepper. Bake until egg whites are set but yolks are mildly running, 15 minutes. (If you prefer a less runny yolk, bake 18-20 minutes.)

Garnish with chives. You can also add sour cream, hot sauce, ketchup, or whatever your family likes. Slice and serve!

Brioche French Toast Casserole

This casserole is a family favorite, I mean people flip out, it's so good. Because it's nice and rich, I often make it for breakfast on the morning of a holiday. Given the fact holiday mornings can be hectic, I usually make this casserole the night before, let it set covered in the fridge, then just throw it in the oven (not literally) in the morning.

Ingredients:
- 1 (16 oz) loaf sliced brioche bread (let this bread sit out overnight to get a little stale, or if you're in a hurry and preparing the day of, lightly toast it at 200°F for 20 minutes)
- 8 eggs
- 3 cups half-and-half
- 2/3 cup packed dark brown sugar
- 1 Tbsp vanilla extract
- 1 tsp cinnamon
- 1/4 tsp salt

Topping:
- 1/2 cup packed dark brown sugar
- 1/2 cup all-purpose flour
- 1/2 tsp cinnamon
- 1/4 tsp nutmeg
- 1/2 cup unsalted butter, at room temperature
- Powdered sugar, for dusting

Directions:
1. Spray a 9"x13" baking dish with cooking spray. Cut the bread slices into quarters to make squares, and arrange them in 4 rows, and along the edge if needed, in the baking dish.
2. Beat the eggs well with an electric or hand mixer. Whisk in half-and-half, brown sugar, vanilla, cinnamon, and salt. Slowly pour over the bread, letting it seep down into the bread. Cover with plastic wrap and let stand at room temperature for 1 hour or overnight.
3. Preheat the oven to 350°F. Prepare the topping: in a small bowl mix together the brown sugar, flour, cinnamon, and nutmeg. Add in the softened butter until the mixture becomes the consistency of peanut butter. Refrigerate until needed.
4. Bake the casserole: remove the plastic wrap from the casserole and crumble the topping over the top of the casserole. Bake, uncovered, for 45-50 minutes or until set. A knife inserted into the center should come out moist, but clean.

Let stand for 20 minutes to rest. Dust with powdered sugar. Serve warm. Enjoy!

Egg-in-a-Hole Breakfast Sandwich

This is a fun breakfast sandwich! When I need to make sure my kiddos are fueled up for a big day ahead, I make egg-in-a-hole breakfast sandwiches. It's pretty qiuick and easy, perfect for weekday mornings when you have a few extra minutes to spare on breakfast. With just a simple touch to transform an ordinary sandwich, your kids will be delighted by the novelty!

Ingredients:
- 2 slices bacon
- 2 slices sourdough bread
- 2 slices cheddar cheese
- 1/2 avocado thinly sliced
- 1 egg
- 1 Tbsp butter
- Kosher salt
- Freshly ground black pepper

Directions:
1. Fry the bacon in a skillet over medium heat until crispy (or use your air fryer). Drain bacon grease and wipe skillet clean.
2. Using a small glass or heart shaped cookie cutter, cut a hole into one slice of bread.
3. Return the skillet to medium heat and add butter. Toast both slices of the bread.
4. Flip bread once golden brown and crack the egg into the hole. Season to taste with salt and pepper. Put cheese, bacon, and avocado slices on the other slice of bread.
5. Cover the skillet and cook until the egg whites are cooked-through and the cheese is melted, about 3 minutes.

Serve and watch 'em smile!

Chapter 8
Odds & Ends

"Honor the Lord with your wealth and with the first fruits of all your crops. Then your barns will fill with plenty, and your vats will overflow with new wine." Proverbs 3:9-10

Some parts of homemaking don't quite fit into tidy categories- but they still matter greatly. They're the quiet rhythms and thoughtful extras that give a home its heartbeat such as setting aside time with the Lord, stirring a pot of jam on a sunny afternoon, composting scraps as an act of stewardship, or simply pausing to light a candle and breathe. This chapter is a gathering place for those meaningful odds and ends- the lovely, practical things that make a mama's everyday life feel rich, rooted, and full of grace.

Daily Quiet Time

I love Proverbs 3:9-10 and reflect on it often. It's commonly applied to a sermon about tithes and offerings, but I think of it in terms of our time, too. In ancient times, crops were the output of an individual's productivity. In this modern day and age, time is our precious commodity. Time can be fruitful, and God asks for our first fruits. I know I've talked a lot about doing more with less and tips to maximize your productivity and bandwidth, and at the same time, I also want to share the importance of a daily quiet time with the Lord. Setting an intention (and an alarm) to set aside five minutes with the Lord each day is really as simple as it seems. Yet so often we are pulled in multiple directions at the same time, and the needs of the here-and-now take over living life in light of eternity as it pertains to our relationship with God. My all-time favorite aid for my daily quiet time with the Lord is *Jesus Calling* by Sarah Young. It's a short, daily devotional incorporating different scriptures into a call from the Lord on your heart. I feel like each time I read the daily devotion, the words leap off the page as if they're written by God, to me, for that day. A good hack to help you put into practice a daily quiet time is putting your devotional on your night stand, and going right to it after you wake up. The five minutes spent reading and praying to the Lord before you even get out of bed for the day makes all the difference!

Getting it All Done

Learning and development is my profession, and as such, I am a huge fan of the late, great Dr. Stephen Covey. Dr. Covey has a now famous analogy for time management. I think about this analogy often and utilize it strategically to help me get it all done.

The analogy is illustrated with a large size glass pitcher, some big painted rocks, and some gravel. Dr. Covey would fill the pitcher with the gravel, then ask someone in the audience at one of his conferences to fit in the rest of the big rocks. These rocks were determined by roles and goals and labeled with things like "children," "spouse," "career," friendships," important projects," "health/fitness," etc. Inevitably, the other person was never able to fit all the big rocks into the pitcher, so they had to choose only one or two of their most important priorities. After this, Dr. Covey would remove the rocks and dump out all of the gravel, but this time, have the other person put the big rocks in first. Then he would pour the gravel back in on top and it would fall over, in between, and under all the big rocks. He would then say, "Prioritize your big rocks first, don't sort gravel." What we can take from this is the idea that our life's priorities are made up of by the roles (and goals) we have. Mine are wife, mother, child of God, professional, cat mama, author, daughter, sister, friend, etc. The highest and best use of our time and the most fulfilling work we will do is when we are putting our effort into a priority, not letting all the other stuff life throws at us distract us from what matters most. Now that can change from day to day depending on the day or the urgency of the moment, but when we apply this to our lives year-in and year-out, we can reap a dividend of intentional living with goals set and met.

Capturing the Memories Created

Years ago, I decided I didn't want time to go by without capturing the memories I and my family have worked so intentionally to create. For my family, this looked like me creating an annual photo album that I give to my husband every year for Father's Day. I utilize iCloud and Shutterfly to make these memory books and then we store them on our coffee table and the bookshelf in our entertainment center. Shutterfly has amazing, complimentary creative design services that I always take advantage of and then finesse the books to my liking. I can't tell you how much it warms my heart to walk out in the morning and see my husband leafing through the pages of our precious memories, for the umpteenth time. Or my little one asking to see the pictures and pointing out each family member she sees on the cover until I can grab my water and sit down with her to show her the pages. These books are dear treasure troves of our life. In case of a fire (God forbid!), I'm grabbing these books. (It is an awesome bonus that Shutterfly keeps these albums stored in your account should you ever need to reprint them).

Lunch Box Notes

With my first child, I wrote lunch box notes on post its and called it a day. But as they say, the more we do something, the better we get at it, so at the time my oldest was outgrowing the lunch box notes, I upped my game for my little one. I always sign her little notes, "Love, mama". I like giving her something that she can keep and put in her backpack or tape to her folder. I've created some lunch box love notes that you can download for free on my website! Go to www.welcomehomebygina.com.

Edible Flowers

I love to include flowers in dishes I prepare. They add novelty and elegance without much effort at all. And typically, they are major crowd pleasers. My 10-year-old eats every single flower that adorns a plate (boys!), although I do not recommend this. I use flowers mainly for their visual aesthetics and to make something look fancier quickly and easily. I'm a visual person, so I've created a chart of just some of the edible flowers you can incorporate into your dishes to elevate even the littlest moments. You can also go to my website and download it for free! www.welcomehomebygina.com.

Drying Flowers

When drying edible flowers and petals for food use (like teas, cakes, syrups, or garnishes), the key priorities are preserving color, flavor, and safety (always use organic / pesticide free).

Here's a short and sweet guide to the best methods for drying edible flowers, along with tips for storage and safety.

1. Air Drying (Gentle & Natural Method)

Best for: chamomile, lavender, calendula, rose petals, thyme blossoms.
Steps:
1. Rinse flowers gently and pat completely dry.
2. Remove excess stems and leaves.
3. Spread petals or whole flowers in a single layer on a paper towel, or drying rack.
4. Place in a cool, dry, shaded area with good air circulation.
5. Let dry for 1–2 weeks, turning occasionally.
6. Store only once crispy and fully dry to prevent mold in an airtight glass container.

This method takes time but requires no special equipment and preserves flavors well.

2. Dehydrator Method (Controlled & Efficient)
Best for: almost all edible flowers.

Steps:
1. Gently clean and dry flowers.
2. Lay flowers or petals in a single layer on dehydrator trays.
3. Set dehydrator to 95-115°F.
4. Dry for 2-6 hours, checking often- flowers should feel papery or crisp.
5. Let cool before storing in an airtight glass container.

This method is faster and more consistent and best if you're drying large batches.

3. Oven Drying (Quick but Risky)
Best for: hardy petals only (i.e., calendula, rose).
Steps:
1. Place flowers on parchment-lined tray.
2. Set oven to lowest setting (ideally around 150°F).
3. Prop the door open slightly to allow moisture to escape.
4. Check every 15-30 minutes. Remove when dry and crisp (usually in 1–2 hours).

Only use for robust flowers, not delicate ones, as there's a risk of discoloration or overheating. Store in an airtight glass jar (not plastic) in a cool, dark cupboard.

Storage Tips

- Label jars with flower name and date.
- Use within 6–12 months for best flavor and color.
- Keep away from heat, light, and moisture.

Flower Press Art

Pressed flower art is a delicate and timeless craft that preserves the natural beauty of blooms by flattening and drying them for use in creative designs. Whether arranged in frames, journals, or handmade cards, each petal and leaf capture a fleeting moment in nature and turns it into lasting beauty. It's a gentle, thoughtful art form that celebrates creation and brings the outdoors into your hands and home. Not to mention, it makes for a wonderful craft to do with the kiddos!

If you are thinking about exploring flower press art, you don't need to invest in a whole host of materials. When I first got started, I just bought some nice paper for my finished product and used pansies from my garden and a hammer from my garage.

Using a piece of parchment paper on top of the flower, stacked on top of your paper, you can literally just tap the pansy with a hammer to press the color out and a beautiful flower will transfer onto your paper. Alternatively, you can go through a specialty shop, such as Modern Pressed Flower (.com) to get a wide variety of materials for use.

Quick Fixes

Have you ever turned on your garbage disposal only to hear that sickening metallic grind, and instantly you know you just tore up a spoon or a fork? Passing on a pearl of wisdom from my domestic maven Aunt Mary Jane, you can use a fine grit sandpaper and go along the edges of your flatware to smooth down the rough bits.

In a household of (only) four people, I am surprised by how many electrical outlets we need. I know you're thinking, just use extension cords or surge protectors…well I did, and then I had an unsightly cordy mess on my hands. It was like a scene out of the movie *The Brave Little Toaster* where the mean vacuum cleaner is chasing the other appliances! Like I've said, I cannot stand visual clutter or disorganization. It truly pains me, so I took care of the problem by buying cord boxes and placing them in just about every room of the house in order to contain the cords and restore peace and sanity. I cannot recommend these enough. You can get them in a few different colors to match your color story, and they're easy to get into and out of.

If you have a fruit tree, you know what it's like to have more fruit than you know what to do with. Like I've said, we have four fruit trees on our property (apple, tangelo, navel orange, and guava), and I can't imagine watching our fruit go to waste. Here are some options you can employ to make the most of your harvests:

1. Seek out recipes for dinners and baked goods that utilize the fruit you have on hand.

2. Dehydrate fruit using a low setting in the oven or a food dehydrating machine. Slice the fruit thin with a mandolin and seal in an airtight jar after. Use the pieces to garnish plated entrees, cocktails or other beverages, salads, etc.

3. We partner with an organization called Food Forward to donate our fruit. You can look them up online at www.foodforward.org, or contact a local food bank in your community in order to donate.

4. Some fruits freeze beautifully without much preparation. You will always need to wash, peel and cut your fruit, then you can freeze it and make smoothies or popsicles out of it, or add it to protein shakes. I have been known to make popsicles for my kids out of almost any kind of fruit; cherries, strawberries, blueberries, oranges (add a little heavy cream, blend, and turn it into an orange creamsicle), lemon, lime, melons, papaya, mango, and more.

5. Another option is to set out a harvest basket for your mail carrier and delivery people. By the same token, you can take a basket into work for your colleagues or drop off fruit to the teachers and administrators at your kids' schools.

Gina Romero

Homemade Jam

Have you ever wondered about the difference between jam and jelly or preserves and marmalade? Jelly is made predominantly from fruit juice and is predictably smooth and firm (due to the sugar content) when spreading.

Jam is made with chopped or pureed fruit, along with fruit juice and sugar, leading to a spread with more texture and fruit pieces, but still smooth enough to spread.

Preserves are made with whole or larger pieces of fruit in a gelled syrup, giving it a chunkier and more fruit-filled texture than jam or jelly.

Marmalade is specifically a citrus fruit preserve, often including chopped citrus peel, resulting in a sweet, sour, and sometimes chewy spread with visible pieces of rind. The most common is made with oranges.

To can jams that you make to give as gifts or preserve for later, cook your mixture to about 220°F on an instant read thermometer, then pour into sterilized jars, and top with new clean lids and rings. Process in a water bath canner (or large, deep pot with a rack on the bottom) for 10 minutes. Allow the jars to sit at room temperature for 24 hours, then store in a cool dry place for 6-10 months. Once opened, refrigerate and enjoy within 2 weeks.

Strawberry Jam

I first made this jam to use as party favors for my daughter's "berry sweet" 2nd birthday party. The aroma this gives off as it cooks is heaven on earth and the finished product was a hit!

Ingredients:
- 1 ½ pints of strawberries
- 1 ½ cups granulated sugar
- 2 Tbsp fresh lemon juice
- 3/4 tsp lemon zest

Directions:
1. Wash and hull strawberries, chop finely.
2. Add to a saucepan and add sugar.
3. Stir over medium heat until incorporated, then bring to a boil and add the lemon juice and zest.
4. Stir continuously at a boil for 12-15 minutes, or until jam reaches 220°F on a food thermometer.
5. Pour into jars and allow to cool to room temperature. Seal and refrigerate.
6. This jam will last up to 2 weeks once opened, in the fridge.

Orange Marmalade

This easy Orange Marmalade recipe is made with only 4 ingredients and is divine! I am always looking for creative and meaningful things to do with our bounty of oranges that ripen each winter, and I can honestly say this is the best orange marmalade! I have used both navel oranges and tangelos for this recipe. You can also store it in the refrigerator for up to 2 weeks or freeze in a freezer safe container for up to 3 months. Prep time: 10 minutes. Cook time: 35 minutes. Total time: 45 minutes. Servings: 6 half-pint Mason jars.

Ingredients:

- About 4-5 medium size oranges (of any variety)
- 1 lemon (juice and zest)
- 1/3 cup water
- 4 cups granulated sugar

Directions:

1. Prep fruit: wash the oranges and lemon, thoroughly scrubbing the peels.
2. Chop: cut off the ends of the oranges. Cut the oranges in half, then cut each half into 4, so you're left with 8 pieces of orange. Discard any seeds.
3. Puree: place the orange pieces in a food processor and pulse/chop until the rind is in very small pieces. Place a plate in the freezer, to help us test for doneness later.
4. Combine in saucepan: add oranges to a large saucepan over medium heat. Zest the lemon into the pot and squeeze the juice from it into the pot. Add water and the sugar and stir well.
5. Cook: bring mixture to a boil. Reduce heat to a low boil and simmer, stirring often, for 30-35 minutes until thickened. When done, it should slide off the spoon in sheets, not droplets, and a spoonful poured onto a cold plate should be a soft gel consistency that moves slightly. If after pouring onto a cold plate it's thin and runs easily on the plate, it is not ready, so continue cooking.
6. Pour into jars or containers with a lid. Allow to cool to room temperature, then store in the refrigerator for up to 2 weeks, or freeze for up to 3 months.

Composting

I love composting. It's actually creative and puts together elements that will meld into a rich, earthen blend of nitrogen and carbon with which you can bless your garden. I also love being able to find something useful to do with my kitchen scraps, and composting helps reduce our waste in the actual kitchen trashcan (something my husband is grateful for). And I'm grateful for being able to save money on bags of topsoil each year.

I do urban composting, as I live in a suburban area of Los Angeles. My yard is neither big, nor small, but I certainly don't have room for a rural type of composting situation. To make composting easy, I keep a bin with a secured lid outside my kitchen door. If you don't have a kitchen door that connects to outside, keep a bin to fill up in your kitchen, under the sink, and take outside once a week to add to your larger compost bin.

Composting can be quite simple, and I find it's best not to overthink it. Your recipe for composting is green (for nitrogen) and brown (for carbon).

Green items: fruits, eggshells, grass clippings.

Brown items: veggies, shredded paper and cardboard (think paper towel and toilet paper rolls), and dead leaves.

Items that have both elements: coffee grounds (and the filter), wood chips, bark, mulch, and old topsoil.

Other items you can add to your compost mixture are breads, crackers, and cereals (hallelujah, there's something useful I can do with the trail of cheerios my little one leaves around my house as though she's a character in Hansel & Gretel), leftover beer and wine, and 100% cottons. Things you should never put in your compost bin are meats, fish, or bones of any kind, dairy of any kind, invasive weeds or diseased or insect ridden plants or clippings.

Compost bins should have a secure lid (I use a bear container on my patio, so I don't attract any unwanted critters). You can compost in both sunny and shady spots, but shade is usually the better choice. While sunlight can speed things up by warming the pile, it can also dry it out quickly- especially in warmer climates. A shady area helps keep your compost moist and provides a more stable environment for the helpful microbes doing all the hard work. Keep your compost bin moist but not soggy by adding water, if needed, when you go to add more scraps. Stir it with a gardening shovel or trowel about once a week or every time you add scraps to it.

Because I am a person who likes to see results, I've developed a schedule that helps me feel meaning behind all the waiting. I anticipate a return on the investment of my time every season, so four times a year. The lag time is the only thing I dislike about composting (it takes weeks to months) for it to mature. However, I have come to appreciate the labor of love my compost goes through to give me roses that burst with splendor and tomatoes that taste like sunshine.

To help you get started, I've created a handy Composting Guide that you can download for free on my website at www.welcomehomebygina.com. Best wishes!

Coming Soon in the *Welcome Home* Series...

Thank you for walking through the rhythms of faith-filled homemaking with me in *Welcome Home*. This journey is just beginning. In the next two books, we'll continue to explore the heart of the Christian home- where Christ is at the center, love is intentional, and everyday life becomes a reflection of grace and beauty.

Coming Next:

Welcome Home: For the Holidays - offering seasonal inspiration, creative ideas, and practical encouragement for cultivating beauty, purpose, and peace throughout the year and in our daily lives.

Welcome Home: Picnics & Parties- filled with delightful recipes, inspirational style, and offering a deeper invitation to embrace each day as a ministry- hospitality becomes worship and homemaking becomes holy ground.

Let's continue to build homes that glorify God in every ordinary and extraordinary moment.

Because a Christ-centered home is not just where we live- it's how we live.

Stay connected at www.welcomehomebygina.com for updates, resources, and release dates.

Reflection Questions

Chapter 1 Reflection Questions

1. **Where do you feel closest to God?**
   Is it in your garden, your kitchen, your morning walk, or somewhere else in creation?

2. **What does "tending garden" look like in your life right now?**
   This could be literal-plants and soil-or symbolic, like nurturing your family, your faith, or your home.

3. **Have you ever experienced God's healing through food or nature?**
   How might you invite more of His goodness into your daily habits and meals?

4. **What are some areas of your life that feel like trial-and-error right now?**
   How can you give yourself the same grace and patience you would give to a garden that's still growing?

5. **When was the last time you slowed down long enough to notice God's beauty around you?**
   How can you make more room for those moments this week?

6. **What one small step could you take to start (or deepen) your gardening journey?**
   Maybe planting herbs in a windowsill, composting, or simply visiting a local nursery to dream.

Chapter 2 Reflection Questions

1. **When have you noticed that clutter or disorder affects your mood or patience at home?**
   How did it make you feel, and what shifted when the space was tidied?

2. **Where in your home do you feel the most peace right now?**
   What makes that space different from other places?

3. **Do you rely on to-do lists or productivity tools?**
   How can you ensure they remain helpful, without becoming idols or sources of stress?

4. **Which of the "household rules" (a place for everything, touch it once, one in/one out, etc.) would make the biggest impact if applied consistently in your home?**

5. **How can you involve your children or family members in maintaining order- without making it feel like a chore?**

6. **What's one area of your home (a closet, a drawer, the kitchen counters) that you can bring order to this week?**
   How might doing so create space for God's peace?

7. **Have you ever experienced spiritual growth through physical order?**
   What lesson did God show you in that process?

8. **How can donating or giving away unused items be not only practical, but also an act of blessing and generosity?** How might you share this message with your children?

Welcome Home: *A Guide to Homemaking From the Heart*

Chapter 3 Reflection Questions

1. **"But as for me and my house, we will serve the Lord." (Joshua 24:15)**
   How does this verse inspire the way you approach your home? What does serving the Lord through your house look like for you?

2. **The Spiritual Side of Design**
   When you walk into your home, does it feel like a place of peace and refuge? If not, what small changes could bring more of God's presence into your space?

3. **Design Principles**
   Which of the Interior Design 101 principles (balance, rhythm, emphasis, proportion, harmony) do you see working- or missing- in your current spaces?

4. **Use of Elements**
   How do color, light, texture, or space influence how you *feel* in your home? Is there one element you could adjust this week to improve the atmosphere?

5. **Purpose of Spaces**
   Think of one room in your house. Does the way you use it align with its intended purpose? How could rethinking its purpose help your family thrive?

6. **Gathering Inspiration**
   Where do you usually find inspiration- Pinterest, magazines, nature, prayer? How could you make your inspiration-seeking more intentional and Christ-centered?

7. **Budget & Stewardship**
   How can you view your design or decorating budget as an act of stewardship, honoring God with your resources?

8. **Personal Style**
   Do you feel pressure to fit into a specific "style box" (modern, farmhouse, etc.), or do you allow your home to reflect your unique story? How might embracing your God-given individuality bring more joy into your design choices?

9. **Eclectic Living**
   What's one meaningful or personal item you'd like to highlight more intentionally in your home? How could it tell part of your family's story?

10. **Hospitality as Ministry**
    How can you use your home- whether big or small, trendy or tired- as a tool for hospitality and ministry this month?

Chapter 4 Reflection Questions

1. **Philippians 4:8-9 Focus**
   When you think about what is noble, pure, lovely, or admirable, how does that apply to the way you care for your home?

2. **Personal Confession**
   Like me, did you "learn" how to clean later in life- or are you still learning? How does grace play a role in your growth as a homemaker?

3. **Tools & Resources**
   What's one tool or resource (Roomba, lint roller, caddies, etc.) you could add or use more consistently to make cleaning easier in your home?

4. **Daily Habits**
   Which of the "house rules" (shoes off, clean tools, paper control, making beds, etc.) could make the biggest difference in your family life if practiced faithfully?

5. **Peace & Atmosphere**
   How do you feel emotionally when your home is tidy versus when it feels cluttered? Can you see a spiritual connection between peace in your home and peace in your heart?

6. **Family Participation**
   How can you invite your children, spouse, or others you may live with into simple daily routines that contribute to a cleaner, more peaceful home?

7. **Methodology**
   Do you tend to "pick a room and finish it" or "pick a task and carry it through the whole house"? Which method works best for your personality and season of life?

8. **Time-Bound Cleaning**
   What's one area you could tackle with a 15–20 minute timer this week? How might that shift the way you view overwhelming tasks?

9. **Faith & Homemaking**
   How does viewing homemaking as your *first ministry* change your mindset about chores and cleaning?

Practical Next Step
What is one small change you can make this week- whether it's a new habit, a decluttered space, or a family rule- that could bring your home more into alignment with God's peace?

Chapter 5 Reflection Questions

1. **Scripture Focus**
   Romans 12:12–13 calls us to *"be joyful in hope, patient in affliction, faithful in prayer. Share with the Lord's people who are in need. Practice hospitality."* Which of these four instructions- joy, patience, prayer, or hospitality- do you most naturally live out? Which one stretches you the most?

2. **Mary & Martha Moment**
   Do you relate more to Mary, who sat at Jesus' feet, or to Martha, who busied herself with serving? How can you cultivate a balance of both "being" and "doing" in your homemaking and hosting?

3. **Heart of Hospitality**
   Think about the last time you hosted someone, whether for coffee, dinner, or overnight. How did your guests feel in your home? How did you feel?

4. **Practical Habits**
   Which of the hosting tips (tone at the door, preparing ahead, creating comfort, being attentive, etc.) could make the biggest difference for you and your family right now?

5. **Ambience and Atmosphere**
   What role do smells, sounds, or small touches (like candles, music, flowers) play in your sense of welcome? Which of these do you enjoy most, and which could you add more of to your home?

6. **Hospitality as Ministry**
   How does thinking of hospitality as a form of ministry change your perspective on opening your home- even when it feels messy or imperfect?

7. **Day-to-Day Hospitality**
   Hospitality doesn't always mean a big event. What are some small, everyday ways you can extend welcome to your family, neighbors, or coworkers this week?

8. **Overnight Hosting**
   If someone were to stay overnight in your home, what little touches would help them feel cared for? How can you prepare in advance so you're not overwhelmed in the moment?

9. **Authenticity vs. Perfection**
   Do you ever hold back from hosting because you feel your home isn't "good enough"? How can you embrace authenticity and warmth instead of striving for perfection?

10. **Personal Challenge**
    What's one step you can take in the next month to practice Romans 12 hospitality- whether it's inviting a neighbor over, preparing a small care basket, or simply greeting your own family with joy?

Chapter 6 Reflection Questions

1. **Scripture Focus**
   Jesus promises in John 14:1-3 that He is preparing a place for us. How does that truth inspire you as you prepare places in your own home?

2. **The Sacred Table**
   What role does the dining table play in your family's life right now? How could you reclaim it as a place of connection, prayer, and beauty?

3. **Everyday Intention**
   Do you tend to view table-setting as "extra work" or as an opportunity for blessing? How might a shift in perspective change this task for you?

4. **Personal Touches**
   Which small detail- place cards, conversation starters, a sprig of greenery, or candlelight- would bring the most joy to your guests? Why?

5. **Seasons of Beauty**
   Which season (spring, summer, fall, winter) inspires you most when it comes to decorating your table? How could you bring that beauty indoors in a simple way?

6. **Faith at the Table**
   How can you incorporate your faith into your meals- through prayer, Scripture, or symbolic touches- that remind guests Christ is the true Host?

7. **Authenticity vs. Perfection**
   Have you ever avoided hosting because your table or home wasn't "perfect"? How might you invite people anyway, with authenticity, warmth, and grace?

8. **Everyday Elegance**
   What's one change you could make this week to elevate your everyday meals- whether using linen napkins, lighting a candle, or setting out flowers?

9. **Table as Ministry**
   Who in your life could be blessed by an invitation to your table? What small step can you take to extend that invitation?

10. **Personal Challenge**
    How will you prepare a place this month- physically or spiritually- that reflects Christ's love and makes room for connection?

Chapter 7 Reflection Questions

Faith & the Kitchen

1. When you think of the verse *"blessed are those who hunger and thirst for righteousness, for they will be satisfied"* (Matthew 5:6), what does that mean for you personally in your kitchen or at your table?

2. In what ways can cooking or preparing food become an act of prayer or worship for you?

Stewardship & Food Waste

3. How do you currently steward food in your home? Are there small changes you could make to reduce waste or to honor God's provision more fully?

4. What emotions do you feel when food is wasted in your home? How might you bring those feelings to God for guidance and peace?

Hospitality & Family Life

5. What does hospitality look like for you in your present season of life? Is it opening your home, making room for family traditions, or simply creating peace for those who live in your home?

6. How can you balance your personal boundaries (like needing space in the kitchen) with the call to serve others joyfully?

Daily Bread & Spiritual Nourishment

7. Jesus calls Himself the "Bread of Life" (John 6:35). What does that truth mean for your relationship with Him right now?

8. Do you ever find yourself turning to food (or other comforts) to fill a need only God can meet? How can you surrender that area of your life to Him?

Practical Living

9. Which of today's tips- whether freezing foods, using an air fryer, or meal planning- could simplify your life and give you more time for what matters most?

10. How might you reframe everyday kitchen tasks as opportunities for gratitude and Christ-like service, rather than chores?

Chapter 8 Reflection Questions

Quiet Time & First Fruits

1. How do you currently give God the "first fruits" of your day?
2. What barriers keep you from setting aside daily quiet time, and how could you remove or work around them?
3. How does starting your day with God affect the rest of your household?

Big Rocks & Priorities

4. What are your "big rocks" right now- your roles and goals that matter most?
5. Where might you be spending too much time on "gravel" tasks instead of focusing on the big priorities?
6. How can you reorder your daily or weekly schedule to better reflect your God-given roles?

Capturing Memories

7. What traditions or memory-keeping practices (like photo books or journals) could help your family remember God's faithfulness over the years?
8. How does pausing to capture memories shift your perspective on the pace of life?

Little Touches of Love

9. What's one small, thoughtful gesture- like a lunch box note or a fresh flower- that you can add to your home life this week?
10. How do little acts of love communicate care and God's presence to your family?

Stewardship & Creativity

11. Where might God be inviting you to steward resources more faithfully- through composting, reducing waste, or repurposing what you already have?
12. How can creativity (crafting, flowers, small fixes) become a form of gratitude in your homemaking?

Hospitality & Grace

13. What simple practice could you add to your home this week that would make it feel more welcoming to your family or to guests?
14. How do you balance striving for beauty with embracing imperfection and grace?

Resources

In an effort to help my fellow mamas, it pleases me greatly to share just a few of the brands, makers, and styles I use and work with, which are available regardless of geographic region.

Aldik Home- a premier destination for luxury home décor, best known for its stunningly realistic artificial flowers, trees, and seasonal displays. With a focus on craftsmanship and elegance, Aldik Home transforms everyday spaces into vibrant, year-round showcases of beauty and style.

Anna Griffin- a renowned designer and entrepreneur known for her elegant, vintage-inspired paper crafting products. With a background in graphic design and a passion for timeless beauty, she has built a beloved brand offering high-quality stationery, scrapbooking supplies, die-cutting tools, and home décor. Her signature style- florals, ornate patterns, and classic motifs- has made her a favorite among crafters who appreciate sophistication, creativity, and a touch of old-world charm. I have been using her cards for years now and I can't recommend highly enough.

Armstrong Garden Centers- a trusted destination for gardeners, offering a wide selection of high-quality plants, expert advice, and garden essentials tailored to California's unique climate. With a legacy of horticultural excellence, they help customers create and maintain beautiful, thriving outdoor spaces. You can also shop online on their website.

Bethany Lowe Designs- renowned for her whimsical, vintage-inspired holiday décor and collectible figurines that capture the charm of bygone eras. Each piece is crafted with nostalgic detail and storytelling magic, perfect for adding a touch of timeless enchantment to any celebration.

B-hyve by Orbit- a smart irrigation system that combines weather-based technology with app-controlled convenience to help you water your garden more efficiently and sustainably. Designed for both residential and commercial use, B-hyve makes it easy to save water, reduce utility costs, and keep landscapes healthy with precision and ease.

Christmas World- a premier destination for festive décor, offering a vast selection of holiday lighting, ornaments, trees, and seasonal displays. Known for its high-quality products and immersive shopping experience, the brand helps customers transform homes, businesses, and events into magical winter wonderlands. Whether traditional or modern, Christmas World provides everything needed to celebrate the season in style, year after year. They are accessible no matter where you live, using their e-commerce site.

Cipriani- a prestigious Italian lifestyle brand renowned for its refined hospitality, timeless elegance, and rich culinary heritage. Originating from the iconic Harry's Bar in Venice- founded in 1931- Cipriani has grown into a global name synonymous with luxury dining, fine Italian cuisine, and sophisticated service. The brand now encompasses world-class restaurants, hotels, event spaces, and gourmet food products, all reflecting its signature blend of simplicity, quality, and understated glamour. I love using their paper products and have found that their product line of napkins offers some of the most unique and beautiful designs out in the marketplace.

Designer's Studio- offers a curated collection of stylish home furnishings, décor, and accessories that blend modern sophistication with timeless charm. Known for their eye for detail and trend-forward pieces, they help transform spaces into beautifully personalized interiors.

Green Thumb- a beloved, family-owned garden center known for its wide variety of premium plants, gardening supplies, and expert advice. With a focus on quality and personalized service, it's a go-to destination for both novice and experienced gardeners looking to grow something beautiful. They carry fabulous Christmas décor and have an e-commerce site set up for easy online ordering.

HeirloomRoses.com- a family-owned nursery specializing in premium, own-root roses grown in the U.S. without harmful chemicals or grafting. They're known for their wide selection of hardy, disease-resistant varieties, and offer everything from classic climbers and fragrant English-style roses to modern hybrids. They have a strong emphasis on quality, sustainability, and expert customer support.

Hester & Cook- a Nashville-based brand celebrated for its artful paper goods and thoughtfully designed home and entertaining accessories. Best known for its signature paper placemats, table runners, and kitchen stationery, the brand combines creativity with everyday function. With designs often inspired by hand-drawn illustrations and vintage charm, Hester & Cook helps elevate everyday dining and special occasions into beautifully stylized experiences. I use their placemats and table décor all throughout the year.

Kurt Adler- a leading holiday décor brand known for its wide array of festive ornaments, nutcrackers, and seasonal decorations. Established in 1946, the company has become a trusted name in Christmas traditions, offering everything from classic and whimsical designs to licensed collectibles. With a commitment to craftsmanship and detail, Kurt Adler brings joy and charm to homes around the world during the holiday season and beyond.

LoveShackFancy Home- brings the brand's signature romantic, vintage-inspired aesthetic into interior spaces with a dreamy collection of textiles, décor, and entertaining essentials. Known for its soft florals, delicate details, and feminine charm, the line features everything from ruffled bedding and heirloom-style tableware to whimsical accents that evoke a sense of timeless elegance and cottagecore beauty. Each piece is designed to create a cozy, enchanting home, filled with storybook charm. They also have a partnership with Pottery Barn which brings me much joy to see two such beautiful worlds collide.

Martha Stewart- my guru. Martha Stewart's brand is a trusted household name synonymous with elegant living, practical know-how, and timeless style. Spanning home décor, cooking, entertaining, gardening, and crafts, her products and content reflect a commitment to quality, creativity, and everyday excellence. With a signature blend of sophistication and accessibility, Martha Stewart inspires millions to elevate their homes and lifestyles with confidence and grace.

Michel Design Works- a Stonewall kitchen brand. Stonewall kitchen makes gorgeous specialty gift baskets, and you can also find their products at your local big box grocery store such as Vons (Safeway) or Ralphs (Kroger). Michel Design Works is known for its beautifully packaged home and gift items that blend timeless elegance with rich, decorative detail. The brand features original artwork and fragrances inspired by nature. Their collections include luxurious soaps, candles, home accents, and stationery. With a focus on quality and design, Michel Design Works brings charm and sophistication to everyday living, making their products popular for gifting and home décor alike. I love that I can incorporate a design for a season and not have to store a bunch of things to achieve the look I want.

Mrs. Alice- a luxury homeware and tablescape brand founded by tastemaker Alice Naylor-Leyland, known for bringing whimsical elegance to entertaining. The brand offers curated collections of tableware, linens, and decorative accents designed to make hosting both effortless and enchanting. With a focus on playful charm, seasonal themes, and timeless sophistication, Mrs. Alice helps transform everyday gatherings into beautifully styled celebrations and quite possibly my favorite aspect is that she creates pieces so unique, you just can't find them anywhere else.

Pottery Barn Kids- timeless, high-quality furniture and décor designed to create magical, functional spaces for children. From cozy bedding and imaginative room themes to durable furniture and personalized gifts, every product is crafted with safety, comfort, and style in mind. With a focus on classic design and lasting quality, Pottery Barn Kids helps mamas build warm, welcoming spaces where childhood memories can be made.

San Antonio Winery- founded in 1917 in Los Angeles, is a historic, family-owned winery and one of the oldest and most beloved in California. Surviving Prohibition through sacramental wine production, it has grown into an award-winning destination known for its rich heritage, hospitality, and diverse wine offerings. With tasting rooms, a full-service restaurant, and a commitment to tradition and innovation, San Antonio Winery offers a warm, authentic experience rooted in over a century of winemaking excellence. They also have a remarkable gift shop on-site and sell their products online as well.

Spode- a historic British brand celebrated for its fine ceramics and iconic blue-and-white patterns, most notably the timeless Blue Italian design introduced in 1816. Founded in 1770 by Josiah Spode, the brand pioneered bone China and underglaze transfer printing, revolutionizing ceramic production. Today, Spode continues to craft elegant tableware and serve ware that blend classic English style with enduring quality- perfect for both everyday use and special occasions. Their Christmas tree pattern, introduced in 1938, has become a beloved holiday classic and a mainstay for Christmases at Casa de Romero. The pattern features a festive evergreen adorned with ornaments and topped by a jolly Santa. The design evokes nostalgic charm and has graced holiday tables for generations, making it a cherished tradition in homes around the world. I just love being able to bring timeless classics into my home to celebrate the season.

The Container Store- where all your dreams come true. Just kidding, but on a more serious note, the Container Store is an incredible Mecca for all, and I mean all of your storage needs. Their innovative storage solutions, from closet systems to pantry organizers, offer stylish and functional products for every room of your home.

Traditions- a charming, family-owned store specializing in year-round holiday décor, offering a magical shopping experience for collectors and festive enthusiasts alike. Located in California, Traditions is known for its curated selection of vintage-inspired ornaments, handcrafted figurines, seasonal decorations, and exclusive artist-designed pieces. Whether celebrating Christmas, Halloween, Easter, or any special occasion, Traditions brings timeless charm and whimsy to every holiday, and I frequent both their retail store and website multiple times a year, as they're always getting amazing new pieces in. I enjoy the thrill of the chase as I curate my seasonal collections year in and year out.

Voluspa- a luxury fragrance brand known for its beautifully crafted candles and home scents that blend exotic ingredients with striking, artful packaging. Founded in California in 1999, Voluspa combines global inspiration with high-quality, sustainable practices—using coconut wax blends and custom-designed vessels. Beloved for its long-lasting scents and elegant presentation, Voluspa transforms everyday moments into sensory experiences. Their candles are truly first rate and their hand cremes are of wonderful quality in feel and scents.

Waterford- a world-renowned luxury brand known for its exquisite crystal craftsmanship, blending Irish heritage with timeless elegance. Founded in 1783 in Waterford, Ireland, the brand is celebrated for its finely cut crystal stemware, home décor, and statement pieces. Synonymous with sophistication and quality, Waterford continues to be a symbol of celebration and refined living around the globe.

Winward Home- celebrated for its luxurious, lifelike home décor and floral arrangements that blend elegance with enduring craftsmanship. Their signature Winward silk florals are meticulously handcrafted to mimic the beauty of real blooms, offering timeless sophistication to any interior space. They are truly the best faux florals I have ever seen.

Acknowledgements

My husband, thank you for loving me so deeply. Thank you for being young at heart and not taking life too seriously. Thank you for supporting this mission of mine, to write this book. It is an honor to raise our children with you. I love you completely.

My son, AJ, there are very few people in this world who can change us at a molecular level. You have done that for me. You are the passion of my life, my pride and joy, the apple of my eye, and the best thing to ever happen to me. I love you with all of my heart.

My daughter, Stella Grace, the Lord bless you and keep you, make his face shine upon you, and be gracious to you. You are breathtaking and precious and I could not imagine my life without you. You are my miracle girl. The happiest day of my life was when I found out I was having a girl- you! I fought for you, God preserved you, and you will do great things in His name. I love you with all that I am.

My mom, Carolyn Herr, who has loved me unconditionally and taught me the value of hard work, among so many other things. Thank you for your support and for your contributions to my life and to my family. And thank you for serving as the Editor of this book.

My stepdad, Dr. Norm Herr, when I think of you, a number of scriptures come to my mind, but I'd like to share this one "He executes justice for the fatherless and the widow, and loves the sojourner, giving him food and clothing" Deuteronomy 10:18. Thank you for taking me in as your daughter, thank you for all of the rich blessings you have bestowed on me. To myself and others, I see you as the greatest example of Jesus's love I have ever met.

My mother-in-law, Karen Dow, who welcomed me with open arms and shared with me her family's favorite recipes.

Courtney Ayotte, who has been by my side since we were thirteen and taught me how to cook several of the recipes in this book.

My Aunt Janice Herr, a professional interior designer who has loved on me, taught me, showed me resources, and has helped me nest some of my most important spaces, as well as plan parties.

Mary Jane Williams, my aunt and a domestic maven from whom I have earned so much.

Pamela Rumph, sister in Christ, and a guru of all things homemaking. Your style, your ideas, your creativity, and your tips have inspired me in ways you wouldn't believe. Thank you.

Martha Stewart, you inspired me from the time I was a young girl with your home making prowess. I wanted to be just like you when I grew up.

About the Author

Gina Romero is a devoted wife, mother, and working professional who has spent years navigating the balance between career and homemaking. With a heart for hospitality and a deep love for Christ, she's passionate about helping women live intentionally and joyfully in the homes God has given them.

Gina is available for author appearances and interviews. For more information, send inquiries to: info@advbooks.com